You Only

A Popular Commentary
and Study Guide on
the Prophecy of Amos

Peter G. Feenstra

www.xulonpress.com

PREFACE

What you find in this book was first delivered in sermon form. I was encouraged by many individuals in my home congregation and elsewhere to put these sermons into print. To make them available and accessible to a wider audience I decided to use the format of a popular commentary and study guide.

This is by no means a professional or scholarly work but has made use of the insights and labours of others. It is my prayer that this book may be productive and fruitful in serving the well-being and edification of Christ's church and the instruction of all who wish to have a deeper understanding of the prophecy of Amos. May the Lord be praised for His gracious love in Jesus Christ through this feeble attempt to explain a portion of His holy and divine revelation.

I wish to thank those who assisted in making this book possible. Many hours of volunteer work were spent on editing, revising, formatting and catching those elusive errors. Special thanks to my loyal and beloved wife Jeanette, my daughter Adena, my friends Glenda Kapteyn and Sharon Pearsons, and to Judy Kingma who affectionately refers to me as her favourite (and only) brother-in-law.

P.G. Feenstra   June 2004

CONTENTS

INTRODUCTION:
ON STUDYING AMOS

*I*n many ways the prophecy of Amos is very contemporary. The issues that the Old Testament church faced have not disappeared over time. As we study this book we have to keep in mind that it is not Amos but the Holy Spirit who is the primary author. We may thank and praise our faithful heavenly Father that He inspired Amos to write down the words of this prophecy for the benefit of the church of all ages and places.

As we delve into the words of this prophecy we discover that faithful Scripture reading, meditation and study are not as easy as they are sometimes perceived to be. The scribes, lawyers and Pharisees in Israel read their Old Testament Bible and thought they were doing well. Nevertheless, Christ rebuked them. He told them that they really did not understand the message of Scripture because they had taken away the key of knowledge (John 5:38-47). The Ethiopian eunuch was riding along in his carriage reading the scriptures. Philip heard him reading from the prophet Isaiah and asked him, "Do you understand what you are reading?" to which the Ethiopian replied, "How can I, unless someone guides me?" (Acts 8:30,31). The true meaning of the passage had to be explained to him.

When we meet together with other Christians to study God's Word we are not simply pooling our resources or sharing opinions and thoughts on a Scripture passage. The task of Bible study is to ascertain the true meaning of Scripture and to understand what the LORD is saying to us in the text.

The Canons of Dort in chapter V article 14 say, "Just as it has pleased God to begin this work of grace in us by the preaching of the gospel, so He maintains, continues and perfects it by the hearing and reading of his Word, by meditation on it, by its exhortations, threats, and promises..." Bible study is extremely important as a means by which we are preserved as children of the LORD.

Before we begin to study Amos we need to humble ourselves before the LORD and pray for insight and knowledge. What we have in front of us is part of God's self-revelation. The prophecy of Amos reveals God to us. The LORD uncovers who He is in His attributes and perfections. Since the LORD is the living God He is revealed to us in His actions. He speaks to His people in language that can be understood so that we might receive an inkling of His ways.

As part of the canon of God's self-revelation, Amos is to be read and studied as the norm and yardstick governing our Christian lives. Through the words of the prophet, the LORD God is speaking to us. What is said has authority. Every aspect of our life must conform and submit to the authority of Scripture including our patterns of worship, social behaviour and care for others in need.

Amos must also be read and studied as redemptive history. Each Bible book, in its own way, demonstrates how our Almighty God and Father labours to place humanity back on the path to full communion with Him. The prophecy of Amos clearly shows us that redemptive history is not all sweetness and light. When the LORD works the redemption of His people, He brings judgment upon the disobedient – on those who turn away from His path. Thus the prophecy of Amos cries out for the coming of Jesus Christ.

Furthermore, the events described in the prophecy of Amos are to be studied from the perspective of God's covenant. Amos is not a story about Israel's failure as such, but reveals the LORD's work with His covenant people. In the Old Dispensation the promise of salvation is given to Israel and Judah. Therefore it is such a terrible offence when Israel disobeys the voice of the LORD. They forfeit the blessings and privileges of the covenant.

Since the covenant relationship between the LORD and His people plays such an important role in the prophecy of Amos, I felt it fitting to select the first two words of chapter 3:2 as the title for this book, "*You only* have I known of all the families of the earth; therefore I will punish you for all your iniquities."

On numerous occasions, reference is made in this study to the book of Deuteronomy. That's because the prophet Amos does not come with a new law but reiterates what was revealed to the people before they entered the land of Canaan. The LORD's warnings and words of judgment are in line with what He spoke through His servant Moses.

Amos is predominantly a sermon of admonition, warning and judgment. Nevertheless, it also announces and alludes to a glorious future for the people of God in the Messiah, our Lord Jesus Christ.

May the LORD bless your study of what He has revealed in the prophecy of Amos. May you see the necessity for a diligent searching of the Scriptures; a study of sustained thought and meditation by which your heart is saturated with the truth of the Bible and "by which the deepest springs of thought, feeling and action may be stirred and directed; the study by which the Word of God will grip us, bind us, hold us, pull us, drive us, raise us up from the dunghill, bring us down from our high conceits and make us its bondservants in all of thought, life and conduct" (John Murray, *Collected Writings.* Vol 1, "The Study of the Bible" p.3).

CHAPTER 1

THE WORD OF THE LORD TO A WAYWARD PEOPLE

Reading: 2 Kings 14:23-29; Amos 7:7-17
Song selection: Psalms 29,33,81,89

Key verses: Amos 1:1,2
The words of Amos, who was among the sheepbreeders of Tekoa, which he saw concerning Israel in the days of Uzziah king of Judah, and in the days of Jeroboam the son of Joash, king of Israel, two years before the earthquake. And he said:
"The LORD *roars from Zion,*
And utters His voice from Jerusalem;
The pastures of the shepherds mourn,
And the top of Carmel withers."

*A*mos, as servant of the LORD, was a messenger of the covenant. What he says was, first of all, a message for his contemporaries. Yet it must be applied by the people of God of all times and dispensations. Amos' prophecy belongs to Holy

Scripture which is "given by inspiration of God, and is profitable for doctrine, for reproof, for correction, for instruction in righteousness, that the man of God may be complete, thoroughly equipped for every good work" (2 Timothy 3:16).

Through Amos the LORD calls us as Christians to have a deeper insight into His ways; to love and obey Him with all our heart, soul, mind and strength and to seek the good of our neighbour. Taking the time to study this Bible book carefully will give you a greater appreciation for God's work of redemption in Jesus Christ. You will see anew the faithfulness of the LORD and the extent of your covenant responsibilities.

It is important to keep in mind that the foundation of Amos' message is the covenant relationship between the LORD and His people. This is not a book appealing for social justice in society at large, but it is a plea for faithfulness, righteousness, justice, and mercy in the church.

In the prophecy of Amos the LORD God of heaven and earth reveals who He is and what He requires of those whom He has set apart to be His people. Our love for Him must be reflected in a love for each other. Such love ought to be based on His love to us, which was shown so marvellously in Christ.

In the early stages of their life as a nation, the LORD had set apart the people of Israel to be His holy covenant people. He had explained how their relationship with Him, and with each other, was to function. He established a beautiful relationship filled with promises and comfort. When the Israelites obeyed the law of the covenant, the LORD favoured them with His blessing. When they forgot the LORD and neglected to fulfil their duties to their neighbours, they were confronted with the curses of the covenant (Deut 27).

The prophecy of Amos speaks powerfully against the social injustices that were present in the community of God's covenant people. The rich were affluent enough to own several homes (3:15) and expensive furniture (6:4). They made sure that they were not denied any satisfaction and pleasure (3:12; 4:1). The poor were abused and exploited at the hands of the rich. Money-making and coveting ruled the day. Both men and women lived for excitement and frivolity (4:1; 6:1-6; 8:5). And as we will see later in this study,

Amos also prophesied against religious formalism and self-willed religion.

WHO WAS THE PROPHET AMOS?

The prophet Amos was a native of the southern kingdom of Judah. We do not know anything about his family background or how old he was when he prophesied. He was not trained as a prophet but was a livestock breeder and cultivator of sycamore trees (7:14). His work would have required him to travel since sycamore trees did not grow anywhere near his hometown.

Amos lived near Tekoa, a village located between Hebron and Bethlehem about 15 kilometres south of Jerusalem. Like all the other sheep-breeders and fruit growers, Amos would have visited the markets that were located in Hebron, Jerusalem, Samaria, and Bethel. At the markets he would have gained some knowledge of the spiritual state of the people.

It is noteworthy that Amos remained a farmer during the time in which he prophesied. He didn't attend a school of the prophets; nor did he receive an income from the work he did as a prophet. Amos was not a "professional" prophet and thus his calling to the office of prophet anticipates and foreshadows the New Testament office of all believers.

Ever since the outpouring of the Holy Spirit on the day of Pentecost, every believer is called to the office of prophet. As we speak in the name of the LORD and proclaim His deeds, we do not change our occupation. We continue doing the work the LORD has given us whether that be at home, on the job-site, or in an office. The calling of Amos to be a prophet of the LORD foreshadows that what was lost in Adam will be regained in Christ.

Believers are members of Christ by faith and thus share in His anointing. An individual does not have to be ordained to the office of minister to speak according to the Word of the LORD. He does not have to go to a seminary to be able to speak out against sin in the church or against injustices and evil in society. He does not need theological training to be able to comfort others with the riches he has in Christ. A child of God can know the will of the LORD without having a Master of Divinity degree. Insight for living is not restricted to those who are ordained to a special office; it is granted to all who open their hearts to the Word of God.

The fact that Amos was and remained a farmer gives a special flavour to the words of his prophecy. When farmers get together they like to compare notes: how the crops are growing, what kind of prices they are getting for their cattle, livestock and for their grain. Amos also knew what it was like to talk about farming. He was in tune with weather conditions and forecasts. Yet he spoke about these matters in a different way than most Israelite farmers did. All matters of farming were seen in the light of God's covenant. He discussed weather patterns in the larger setting of what the LORD was saying and doing. The believing farmer recognized these things come from the LORD "who is wonderful in counsel and excellent in guidance" (Isaiah 28:29).

As Christians we too are prophets. That position should be obvious in how we talk about climate and weather conditions. More often than not people will talk about the weather within its own frame of reference. The secularism of our day explains weather patterns in terms of cause and effect. No thought is given to what the LORD God might be telling us when floods devastate one area of the world and drought causes suffering in another. Not even the *Farmers' Almanac* takes the providence of God into account when making its forecasts. We who have been called to the office of prophet must learn to speak about the weather, about sales and pricing, about business and commerce, about exams and learning as those who are being taught by the Word of the LORD.

IT SEEMED TO BE THE BEST OF TIMES

Amos was from a small town in Judah, but he was sent with a powerful message from the LORD to the ten northern tribes of Israel. These tribes had broken away from Judah after the death of Solomon. During the reign of Solomon's son, Rehoboam, the kingdom was divided into two parts. Judah continued to exist in the south ruled by kings in the line of David.

The Northern kingdom went its own way under the leadership of various kings. The first of these kings was Jeroboam the son of Nebat. Jeroboam I put politics and the economy of the nation above the service of the LORD. To keep the Northern kingdom intact, he decided to establish two centres of worship – one in Dan and the other in Bethel. In this way the people of the ten tribes had no reason to go to the Southern kingdom or to worship in Jerusalem. Thus the people of the North were led away from the true service of the LORD and from the place God had chosen in Jerusalem.

Israel was hemmed in by neighbouring kingdoms during the first years of its separate existence. There were frequent border skirmishes with Syria and Judah. Economically and politically, times were tough. From the reign of Jeroboam the son of Nebat to the arrival of Jeroboam II, Israel was not living in the best of times.

All of that changed by the time Amos arrived on the scene. Amos lived about 750 years before Christ's coming in the flesh. We read in 1:1 that he spoke the Word of the LORD during the reigns of Uzziah (791-740 BC) and Jeroboam II (793-753 BC). Uzziah was king over the Southern kingdom of Judah and Jeroboam II ruled over the Northern kingdom of Israel from his headquarters in Samaria.

By worldly standards, Jeroboam II was a very successful king. He knew what he was doing and read the political situation well. Jeroboam II expanded the borders of Israel so that they possessed much the same territory they did when Solomon was on the throne. There was peace between the Northern kingdom of Israel and Judah during his reign. The old hostilities subsided. The nation of Israel enjoyed a period of political peace and even a measure of international prestige.

On the international scene, Egypt and Babylon were weak. Syria (Aram), which had given Israel much trouble, had been subjugated by the king of Assyria. The kingdom of Assyria was having its own troubles and was not in any position to threaten Israel.

Jeroboam II ushered in a period of wealth and prosperity such as Israel had not known before. Riches accumulated rapidly. Many were wealthy enough to maintain both a winter home and a summer home (3:15). They slept in beds of ivory and ate the most expensive foods. The people basked in wealth that even some foreign kings did not possess.

Everything appeared to be in good order – also when it came to matters of religion and worship. Large groups of pilgrims travelled through the land to visit the shrines and holy places. The religious centres were abuzz with people sacrificing an abundance of offerings. Never were so many voluntary sacrifices made. Chapter 4:4,5 alludes to this, " 'Come to Bethel...to Gilgal and bring your sacrifice of thanksgiving of that which is leavened, and proclaim freewill offerings, publish them; for so you love to do, O people of Israel!' says the LORD God." For all intended purposes it looked as though the LORD was really blessing the northern tribes. Indeed, it seemed to be the best of times — a great time to be alive.

IT REALLY WAS THE WORST OF TIMES

Although outwardly everything looked beautiful, Israel was rotten to the core spiritually. It seemed as though it was the best of times but, in fact, it was the worst of times. While the people enthusiastically upheld the rituals and traditions of worship, they in fact trampled upon the covenant, failing to love the LORD with all their heart, mind, and strength. Israel's prosperity was not the result of their faithfulness, or the intelligence of Jeroboam, but was because of the LORD's compassion and longsuffering. For years they had been oppressed but now under Jeroboam II God granted relief. As we read in 2 Kings 14:26,27, "For the LORD saw that the affliction of Israel was very bitter; and whether bond or free, there was no helper for Israel... but He saved them by the hand of Jeroboam the son of Joash." The LORD in His compassion, longsuffering and forbearance gave His people another opportunity to repent and amend their ways. Economic prosperity does not necessarily mean a people is being blessed. Israel's prosperity witnessed of the LORD's patience and would one day testify against them.

Israel's worship was self-willed and a mere formality. The rich cared only about becoming richer and neglected the poor. As long as they maintained their standard of living, what did they care about others in the communion of saints? They trampled upon the poor, demanding high interest rates on the money people owed them. The merchants used false weights and measures in their business transactions. They could hardly wait until sundown on the Sabbath day so that they could get on with life and could get back to making money. Their minds were on their work even as they worshipped. Both men and women indulged in loose living and drunkenness as though this was what made life worth living. And, in the meantime, they piously sang the psalms of David.

Furthermore, Israel ignored God's standards for holy living. Authority was despised (5:10,12) and the leaders of the nation sought publicity and prestige. Moral standards were virtually non-existent. Sexual indulgence was accepted. Personal likes and dislikes became the norm for living (2:7; 6:4-6).

Those to whom Amos spoke felt quite at ease. They adored traditional and "old-time" religion, but, in reality, they had cut themselves loose from the Word of the LORD. Hardened in unbelief, these people did not fear the day of the LORD. They felt secure in being the chosen people of the LORD, so what could go wrong? Israel believed God's punishment would only come upon the heathen.

The LORD, however, sends Amos to call Israel to repentance and to warn of impending judgment. God says, as it were, "This cannot and will not continue." The people of Israel must repent of their sins lest they, too, fall under the wrath of the LORD. Amos must proclaim where true life and wealth can be found – in the unadulterated ministry of reconciliation. Before they are punished, the people of God must hear why the LORD is angry with them.

The formulation of chapter 1:1 is rather remarkable. You would expect it to read, "The words of Amos...which he *heard* concerning Israel." Instead we read, "The words of Amos...which he *saw* concerning Israel." That means the word Amos proclaims touches him deeply. He sees the truth and the power of the words he speaks. Amos sees where the LORD will lead His people. If there is no repentance, judgment will come. The LORD has spoken and He will do it. His word is powerful, trustworthy, and living. The LORD Himself empowers Amos and gives him authority to speak on His behalf.

The Great Shepherd sends Amos because the sheep must hear His voice. The LORD does not speak in a still, small voice but He roars like a lion. The roar of a lion, locked up in a zoo, already sends shivers down our spines. But return a lion to its natural habitat and you have a portrait of God. "Roaring" is a ferocious word which depicts approaching destruction and death (Motyer, p.27).

The very first word that crosses the lips of the prophet is the covenant name of God: Yahweh. The LORD who revealed Himself as the God of deliverance (Exodus 3) now approaches His people in covenant anger and judgment.

Notice from where the voice of the LORD is heard! The LORD roars like a lion *from Zion*. He utters His voice *from Jerusalem*. The word of the LORD thunders from the city of God. His voice does not come forth from Dan or Bethel, the centres of worship the Israelites have constructed for themselves, but from the place the LORD Himself had chosen as His dwelling place. Judgment will not only *come* upon the house of the LORD, but it will *begin* there (Ezekiel 9:5,6; 1 Peter 4:17).

In the Old Dispensation, Zion and Jerusalem became the symbols of God's government and of true worship. God's voice came forth from Zion (for example, Psalms 48, 122, 147). In the prophecy of Amos, the LORD declares war against those centres of worship that deny His rule and His government. He will show His disobedient children that they may not go their own way, separating themselves from the place where the glory of His name is proclaimed.

Salvation will come forth from Zion and from the land of Judah. Yet redemption and deliverance are not for those who continue to live in sin and ignore the covenant God established with them. The LORD will punish those who worship Him in their own self-willed manner. Amos, a shepherd by trade, warns the flock of God's pasture that they are in real danger of being consumed by the Lion of the tribe of Judah. They will be devoured by the wrath of the LORD if they do not repent.

The judgment of the LORD will be all-inclusive and total. From the fertile valleys (the pastures of the shepherds) to the height of Carmel (the place where the LORD revealed Himself to be the only true God – I Kings 18:38,39) the wrath of God will be experienced.

It did not take long before the people saw the beginning of the end. Two years after Amos prophesied, Israel was hit by a devastating earthquake. Earthquakes in the Old Testament were a prophetic sign of God's impending judgment. They were (and still are) meant to draw people's attention to the day of judgment!

Thus the addition, "two years before the earthquake," is more than a historical detail. It underlines the power of the prophet's words. It was so devastating that 200 years later the prophet Zechariah also mentions this very same earthquake (Zech 14:5). People remembered the earthquake as an act of divine judgment.

Shortly after Amos prophesied, the world of prosperity and economic growth began to unravel for the Northern kingdom. The first sign of judgment was the earthquake. Less than forty years later, the nation was carried off into captivity.

APPLICATION FOR OUR TIMES

Today we live in prosperity – and again it seems to be the best of times. But let us not fool ourselves. Corruption and immorality are all around us. We are heading for destruction, also as a church, if moral absolutes and the ordinances of the covenant are classified as matters of private opinion. A congregation can only be assured that it will escape the judgment of God when it continues to submit itself to the authoritative standard of the Word of the LORD and seeks its life in Christ.

Our God is an awesome God. He shows mercy to thousands of those who love Him and keep His commandments, but He will by no means clear the guilty. One day He will once again roar from Zion and He will shake both heaven and earth (Hebrews 12:22-29). Therefore we must stand in awe of Him and worship Him as He has commanded in His Holy Word. The more we know, the more we will be held accountable (Hebrews 10:26-31).

Through the preaching your eyes are opened to what you have in Christ. Let the message of the gospel never testify against you. You know who God is! Listen to His voice and live!

Questions

1. The prophecy of Amos has its own place in redemptive history. What does the LORD reveal about Himself in this

book?

2. Amos was a farmer from Tekoa. How does his agricultural background flavour the language of this prophecy? Give examples.

3. Why did the LORD pick a prophet from Judah to preach to the Northern kingdom of Israel?

4. Why is the king of Judah mentioned in verse 1 when the prophecy of Amos is directed at the people of the Northern kingdom of Israel?

5. How does Amos' calling as prophet serve as a foreshadowing of our task as prophets of the LORD? How are we to fulfil our prophetic calling today?

6. How can we witness of God's providence and His covenant faithfulness through the manner in which we speak about the weather?

7. Why does Amos use the image of the LORD roaring like a lion?

8. Why do both salvation and judgment begin in the church?

9. What does it mean to be blessed by the LORD? How can economic prosperity and success in business be a curse rather than a blessing? (see also Psalm 73, Psalm 127 and Heidelberg Catechism Lord's Day 50).

10. Look up other passages of Scripture that refer to earthquakes. Discuss the significance of earthquakes in the light of God's redemptive acts.

CHAPTER 2

JUDGMENT ON TWO BLOOD BROTHERS

Reading: Amos 1:3-2:11; Obadiah
Song selection: Psalms 94,98,108,137,149

Key verses: Amos 1: 11-15

Thus says the LORD:
"For three transgressions of Edom, and for four,
I will not turn away its punishment,
Because he pursued his brother with the sword,
And cast off all pity;
His anger tore perpetually,
And he kept his wrath forever.
But I will send a fire upon Teman,
Which shall devour the palaces of Bozrah."

Thus says the LORD:
"For three transgressions of the people of Ammon, and
for four,
I will not turn away its punishment,

Because they ripped open the women with child in Gilead,
That they might enlarge their territory.
But I will kindle a fire in the wall of Rabbah,
And it shall devour its palaces,
Amid shouting in the day of battle,
And a tempest in the day of the whirlwind.
Their king shall go into captivity,
He and his princes together,"
Says the LORD.

The terms "judgment" and "punishment" are not exactly popular in mainstream Christianity. "Hell" and "damnation" are words most people would relegate to a time when preachers delivered "hell, fire and brimstone" sermons (J. Arnold p. 25).

Amos 1:11-15 deals with punishment and judgment. The LORD in burning wrath and anger will consume those who do not honour or obey His Word. As we study these verses we need to keep in mind that there is a progression in the LORD'S anger over sin. It is worse for a covenant child to defy the living God than it is for an unbeliever. Those who reject God's statutes and ordinances in the New Testament receive a more severe punishment than those in the Old Dispensation.

To give one example: Edom is condemned for his anger against his brother, Israel. While the LORD speaks of fire consuming the Edomites, Jesus Christ speaks of the fire of hell that will sweep over those in the church who are not reconciled to their neighbour, "But I say to you that whoever is angry with his brother without a cause shall be in danger of the judgment. And whoever says to his brother, 'Raca!' shall be in danger of the council. But whoever says, 'You fool!' shall be in danger of hell fire" (Matthew 5:22).

Scripture repeatedly speaks of the judgment of God upon those who do not serve the LORD as He has commanded in His Word. God is love, but He is also a consuming fire. The LORD'S warning about the coming day of judgment belongs to the good news of salvation because it will be the day when Jesus Christ will grant us full redemption from sin.

The punishment of the LORD upon those nations mentioned in Amos 1 is a prelude to the final day of judgment. The enemies of the cross will be destroyed and cast into everlasting hell where they will never again be allowed to tamper or ruin what God has created beautiful.

Even though the nations have not received the special revelation of the LORD they are without excuse. They are held accountable for their actions (Psalm 19:1; Acts 14:17; 17:28; Romans 1:19-23; Romans 2:14,15).The nations violate all the commandments of God's law. It is rather striking, however, that the sins which Amos condemns involve the second part of God's law – the duties we owe our neighbour. The people of Israel must be punished because they have committed extreme, barbaric deeds of cruelty and sickening acts of atrocity (e.g., 1:3,13).

THE CONTEXT OF GOD'S JUDGMENT

The manner in which chapter 1:11-15 is structured is part of a pattern which began in chapter 1:3. Eight times we read the phrase, "Thus says the LORD: 'For three transgressions of ...and for four, I will not turn away its punishment, because ...'" These words are like a roll of thunder warning that a storm is quickly approaching. Nation after nation hears how the LORD God of the covenant will not allow them to go their own way. He will punish their sin and transgression.

The repetition of the phrase "for three transgressions ... and for four" refers to sins that are multiplied, which have become a way of life for those who do them. The LORD is not speaking out against those who may fall into a particular sin once or even twice. He is not lashing out against individuals who struggle against daily sins of weakness. Our covenant God shows mercy and compassion to those who hate sin and are grieved by its presence in their lives, yet who fall into it. God's wrath is directed against those who harden themselves in sin and who enjoy *living* in sin. The fourth transgression quickly follows on the heels of the third violation because sin has become a lifestyle.

The Word of the LORD applies not only to the chosen people but to all nations under heaven. The LORD is God of all nations. Amos proclaims God's Word to the nations in a very interesting way. Picture, if you will, the eight countries in rings around a circle. Each nation has a specific place within the rings. The Northern kingdom of Israel is at the centre of the circle. The other seven nations are located around the centre of the circle. Amos starts with the nations that are the furthest removed from Israel. With each message the prophet moves in closer to the centre of the circle.

The first three messages are directed to nations that are on the outer edges of the circle. These nations are: Syria, Philistia and Tyre. God will judge Damascus (the capital of Syria) for its cruelty. Philistia is judged by God because the people have participated in slave trading. Tyre is condemned because it does not keep the promises it makes to others. Closer to the centre are the nations of Edom, Ammon, and Moab. These nations are blood-brothers of Israel. We will return to them in the next section.

The words of judgment do not end here. The circle of judgment closes in on Israel. Now it is the turn of her southern sister, Judah. Even though Judah received the covenant promises of the LORD she is no better than the pagan nations, because "they have despised the law of the LORD, and have not kept His commandments. Their lies lead them astray, lies which their fathers followed" (2:4).

The people of the Northern kingdom of Israel were quite pleased with the prophet from Judah as long as he was talking about other nations. They listened with a self-satisfied attitude, "Well, they received what was coming to them." Their celebration is cut short, however, as Amos continues speaking words of judgment against Israel. For the circle of judgment draws closer and finally tightens like a rope around Israel's own neck. When the prophet points the finger at them, they become angry and say, "Why don't you go away and preach someplace else?"

Do you understand the context of the judgments of the LORD against Edom, Ammon and Moab? There is a progression from bad to worse. What Syria, Philistia, and Tyre did was bad, what Edom, Ammon and Moab did was worse, but the sins of Judah and Israel were the worst of all! No sin is more offensive than breaking covenant with the LORD God through disobedience and self-willed worship. The lightning of God's wrath will strike the people of God the hardest.

It's easy for people to talk about how bad things are in other churches and in society in general. We tend to turn things around and think the sins of others are worse than our own and the crimes of society are worse than those committed within the church. But that is not true!

As we read about the LORD's judgment upon those outside the church we shouldn't sit back and feel complacent or comfortable. For the judgment of the LORD begins with us. That's the centre of the circle. When judgment comes upon others it is always meant as a warning for us.

THE LORD JUDGES THE ANGER OF EDOM

The first blood-brother to be judged is Edom. The LORD has kept track of the sins of Edom. Edom is condemned because he is constantly angry with his brother. He refuses to be reconciled and continues to hold a grudge. This hatred began already when Jacob received the blessing from Isaac and his brother Esau did not. Esau was hostile to Jacob even in the womb, and these feelings were passed on from one generation to the next. Amos says that Edom "pursued his brother with a sword, stifling all compassion because his anger raged continually and his fury flamed unchecked" (NIV).

The LORD considers this offence to be so detestable that the entire book of Obadiah is concerned with it. We read, for example, "For violence against your brother Jacob, shame shall cover you, and you shall be cut off for ever. In the day that you stood on the other side – in the day that strangers carried captive his forces, when foreigners entered his gates and cast lots for Jerusalem, even you were as one of them. But you should not have gazed on the day of your brother in the day of his captivity; nor should you have rejoiced over the children of Judah in the day of their destruction; nor should you have spoken proudly in the day of distress" (Obadiah 1:10-12).

God's wrath is roused when brothers quarrel and cannot get along together. The LORD condemns all enmity and strife between brothers because hatred is contrary to His nature. Look where it leads when brothers do not dwell in unity. It can result in hatred that is perpetuated for generations. The fathers pass it on to the children and the children to their children.

Edom will be punished because he has let the sun go down on his anger. Thereby he has become an instrument in the service of the devil and not for the coming of the Messiah. In fact, he opposes the coming of the Messiah.

Centuries earlier, the LORD called Abraham because of His desire to form a covenant people for Himself, a nation that would receive a glorious heritage. The Messiah and Saviour of the world would be born from this nation. The love of the LORD for His people Israel manifested itself in the home of Isaac and Rebecca. Two boys were born in that family but Jacob is preferred above Esau not because Jacob was a better person but because he was chosen to bear the messianic promises. Although God's electing love called Jacob to be the one from whom the Messiah would be born, both were required to walk in the light of His word. Only in the obedience of faith could both Jacob and Esau participate in the promises of God.

The LORD in His sovereign good pleasure decides whom He will use to bring about the coming of His Son. Israel is the people of the LORD from whom the Messiah will be born. Therefore Scripture says, "Jacob I loved but Esau I hated." This did not mean that no one in Edom could be saved, but God chose Jacob's descendants to be the bearers of the promise. Yet Esau did not want to be subject to the sovereign will of the LORD. That refusal manifests itself when Jacob and Esau develop into nations. The Edomites do not submit themselves to the sovereign counsel and plan of the LORD but do everything to oppose the people of God.

Edom tried to stop the Israelites on many occasions. It began when Israel came into Canaan. From that point on they were constantly at war with Israel. Wasn't Herod, who was responsible for the slaughter of the children of Bethlehem, an Idumean, that is, an Edomite and a descendant of Esau? The slaughter of the children of Bethlehem was the ultimate outcome of Edom's unchecked fury and hatred against the people of the LORD. Thus the LORD says, "I will send a fire upon Teman, which shall devour the palaces of Bozrah" (1:12). Teman was a district in Edom that apparently produced many leaders and was known for its wisdom. Eliphaz, one of Job's friends, came from this area (Job 2:11). Not only will wisdom depart from Teman (Jeremiah 49:7), all of Edom, from Teman in the east to Bozrah in the west, will go up in flames. They will not escape the punishment of the LORD.

The root of the antagonism between Edom and Israel is the enmity between the seed of the serpent and the seed of the woman. The wrath of Edom stems from the antithesis between the church and the world. Once we realize this we will understand why the hostility does not end.

The punishment of Edom was a warning to those who heard the word of the LORD. The covenant people in the Northern kingdom did not acknowledge the sovereign work of the LORD in choosing Jerusalem as His dwelling place and in choosing Judah as the tribe from whom the Messiah would be born. Like Edom, they had no business separating themselves from the people of God or from the true worship of His name for political, economic or other reasons.

Is this not a warning for us also? The LORD calls us to acknowledge His sovereign ways and good pleasure in how He gathers His people. We may not separate ourselves from the true worship of His name for the sake of convenience, work, vacation or other reasons. How often do you not see it happen that those who separate themselves from the true worshippers of God develop an unrestrained hatred for those who seek after righteousness and truth?

THE LORD JUDGES THE CRUELTY OF AMMON

Ammon is the second blood relative to be spoken against. A dark cloud of iniquity hangs over the origin of this nation. Ammon together with Moab was conceived and born in a most terrible situation of fornication (Gen 19:30-38). It is a shameful story that is stained with drunkenness and immorality.

Ammon and Moab were born to the daughters of Lot. They made their father commit an immoral act with them after they had made him drunk. Thus Lot was both the father and grandfather of Ammon. The sin the daughters of Lot committed with their father demonstrated rather clearly that the environment in which a person lives isn't neutral.

These daughters of Lot became accustomed to a sinful lifestyle because of what they saw while living in the land of Sodom. They shook off all feelings of guilt and shame and became calloused and insensitive to sin. This was the way Ammon was born into the world and it became a pattern of life for the entire nation of Ammon. The sins of the fathers were passed on to the children. In cold-blooded murder, the people of Ammon seized pregnant women and ruthlessly cut them open. They did this because they were obsessed with power and enlarging their borders. They did not fight against other nations in self-defence or to liberate themselves from their enemies but they wanted more power. The Ammonites believed the best way of attaining their goal was by killing every Israelite including the unborn children.

We should not forget who was behind the actions of Ammon. Satan was trying to destroy the seed of the woman. If only he could prevent the Messiah from being born, he could be king of the world. Therefore, as on other occasions, he attacks the unborn children.

In the battlefields of Gilead, where pregnant women were being mercilessly murdered, there was a battle taking place which was not a war of flesh and blood (Ephesians 6). This was what John would see in his vision while on the island of Patmos as recorded in Revelation 12. The apostle saw a dragon standing before the woman ready to devour her child. The devil always wanted to take the child away from the woman, and Christ away from His church. It was the dragon who stood before the women of Gilead, seeking to devour their children. In this, too, Satan attempted to destroy the coming of Christ. What the Ammonites did wasn't just an attack on another nation, but was also an attack on the work of the LORD. Therefore He will not hold them guiltless.

Such is the case today as well. Most people would condemn what the Ammonites did and they would consider it cruel, barbaric, distasteful and sickening. Our society is too civilized to treat pregnant women in such a shocking and disgusting manner! Yet the sin of Ammon lives on in the millions of abortions that have taken place around the globe and within our own country. We have the medical know-how and technology to snuff out the life of the unborn without killing mothers, but the result is still the same.

Ammon killed women and children of Gilead because of their obsession with power. Today unborn children are killed because they are inconvenient. They fall victim to the selfish pursuits of men and women who live without God.

Do you think the LORD, who punished the Ammonites for the atrocities they committed, will let our society go unpunished? Certainly not! He who kindled a fire on the wall of Rabbah and devoured the strongholds of Ammon will punish the godlessness of our society with the fire of hell. Therefore today, in the office of prophet, we not only have a duty to oppose abortion but we must warn all those who commit similar sinful practices that they will not escape the punishment of the LORD. All government officials and citizens who defy the ordinances of our God will feel the heat of His anger on that day when He comes to judge the living and the dead. For three transgressions and for four our society is ripe for judgment. The LORD will not revoke the punishment.

In Christ and in Him alone we find our consolation and certainty. We are involved in the process of the ingathering of the church. In Christ and in what He is doing in His church there is hope for the nations! There is a glorious prospect for those who cling to Jesus Christ with a true and living faith and who find shelter under the shadow of the LORD's wings. By God's grace they are freed from wrath through the work of Christ.

As we see the judgments of the LORD on the nations let us never gloat or think they deserve it more than we do. For if this is the judgment that is coming upon those who live outside the church of Christ, you can count on it that the punishment will be more severe against those who know the LORD but spurn His love. There remains a fearful prospect of judgment and a fury of fire (Hebrews 10:26-31). Let each of us repent of our sins and humbly seek our life apart from ourselves in Christ. Christ took the burden of God's wrath caused by our sin upon Himself. He will show His mercy to those who love Him and keep His commandments.

Questions

1. What is the historical background of each of the nations that are mentioned in chapter 1:3-2:11?

2. What message is conveyed by the repeated phrase, "For three transgressions of ... and for four, I will not turn away its punishment, because ...?" Is there any significance in the numbers three and four?

3. What are the specific sins that lead the LORD to punish the nations that are mentioned? Are there some sins which are more disturbing to the LORD than others?

4. Think of other examples in Scripture where individuals were quick to criticize and highlight the sins of others but refused to see their own sins. How is this condemned by our Lord Jesus Christ?

5. What do we learn from the life of Esau about the implications of being a member of God's covenant people? What does this tell us about the relationship between covenant and election?

6. May someone say, "Even though I have been baptized I don't think I'm a child of the LORD. Does it matter how I live?"

7. Cite examples from Scripture and history that show the worst persecution often comes from those who at one time belonged to the community of believers.

8. How could our environment have a negative affect on us? Are there ways in which we can avoid such influences?

9. What is the proper Christian response to abortion? Is it really a matter of a "right to life?" In light of what we read in Romans 1:18-32 why should it not surprise us that so

many abortions have taken place?

10. How can we effectively warn the citizens of our country and fellow Christians regarding the evil of abortion?

11. As New Testament believers we are more accountable for what we know than Old Testament believers. Discuss what this means. How will this affect the manner in which we read and apply the narratives of the Old Testament? Explain your answer with an Old Testament example.

12. The people of Moab were punished by the LORD because they burned the bones of the king of Edom to lime (2:1). Why was this such a serious offence?

CHAPTER 3

THE PUNISHMENT OF THE LORD UPON THE NORTHERN KINGDOM OF ISRAEL

Reading: Ephesians 5:1-20
Song selection: Psalms 72,101,107,119,146

Key verses: Amos 2:6-12
Thus says the LORD:
"For three transgressions of Israel, and for four,
I will not turn away its punishment,
Because they sell the righteous for silver,
And the poor for a pair of sandals.
They pant after the dust of the earth which is on the head
of the poor,
And pervert the way of the humble.
A man and his father go in to the same girl,
To defile My holy name.
They lie down by every altar on clothes taken in pledge,
And drink the wine of the condemned in the house of
their god.

"Yet it was I who destroyed the Amorite before them,
Whose height was like the height of the cedars,
And he was as strong as the oaks;
Yet I destroyed his fruit above
And his roots beneath.
Also it was I who brought you up from the land of Egypt.
And led you forty years through the wilderness,
To possess the land of the Amorite.
I raised up some of your sons as prophets,
And some of your young men as Nazirites.
Is it not so, O you children of Israel?"
Says the LORD.
"But you gave the Nazirites wine to drink,
And commanded the prophets saying,
'Do not prophesy!'"

*I*n Romans 12:2 the LORD calls all those who hear the message of the gospel to live in holiness. "And do not be conformed to this world, but be transformed by the renewing of your mind, that you may prove what is that good and acceptable and perfect will of God." Many times we, as Christians, either knowingly or subconsciously let ourselves blend in with the rest of society. How different are our attitudes from others in our community? Do we live a distinctively Christian lifestyle? We will not deny being Christian, yet no one, whether adult or teenager, relishes the thought of being different. We would rather "fit in" with the mainstream of society.

The desires of our sinful nature easily ensnare us to follow the fads and trends of society blindly, without considering their influence on us and our children. The very same tongue which offers praise to God on the Lord's Day often becomes vulgar and foul the moment we step into the workplace. The music fostered by a world of paganism seems to be more appealing than the songs which praise and honour the LORD.

World conformity does not just happen. There is a process in which individuals, families and churches gradually fall away from the true service of the LORD. The first step is that you are no longer sure why you believe what you believe. You maintain a certain form of worship because this is what you have grown used to. You follow a particular pattern taught by your parents without knowing why you do it. You worship God out of custom or tradition but not with your heart, nor with conviction. Before long, you no longer know what you believe and the end result is that you no longer care.

True believers are not to be like chameleons who change colour to fit in with their surroundings. A "camouflaged Christian" has no defence against his three sworn enemies – Satan, the world, and his own sinful flesh. What we have in Christ should stir us up to a life of holiness. We have been delivered from darkness to walk as children of light; we have a calling to be different.

The prophet Amos spoke out against those in the Northern kingdom of Israel who attempted to camouflage themselves and blend in with the secular world around them. His contemporaries acted in much the same fashion as the heathen nations, as those who did not know the LORD. The path they were treading was very dangerous. It would lead them to their own demise, destruction and ruin. Through what Amos proclaims in chapter 2:6-12 we hear the Holy Spirit calling all God's people, both of that time and now, to repent and live for the LORD.

THE VIOLATION OF GOD'S JUSTICE FOR THE POOR

In message after message, Amos pronounces God's judgment upon the nations that surround Israel. Seven times Amos' audience hears him proclaim, "Thus says the LORD: 'For three transgressions of...and for four, I will not turn away its punishment; because...'"

There are several reasons why Israel must hear the judgment of the LORD on Judah before they find out what He has to say to them. First, the people of the Northern kingdom of Israel must realize that the prophet Amos isn't singling them out. Amos isn't opposed to the fact that, since the days of Jeroboam I, Israel has gone its own separate way both politically and economically. He makes known to them the LORD's judgment on Judah to point out to the Northern kingdom that the LORD shows no partiality.

When the people of God are not diligent in fulfilling their God-given task they will start doing what the LORD forbids. Israel must know this is where Judah is at as well. They, too, have rejected the law of the LORD and have not kept His commandments.

From chapter 2:6-9:10, the attention is no longer on others. The full fury of the storm of God's wrath now hits the Northern kingdom of Israel. The LORD will not hold them guiltless since they do not respect His statutes and ordinances. On the Sabbath Day they go through all the rituals of worship and outwardly it looks wonderful, but their daily conduct is no different from that of the surrounding nations.

Amos charges the Northern kingdom of Israel with seven counts of sin – a number indicating their sin has reached its full measure. The first four charges and the sixth one involve the manner in which they treat those who are less well off. "They sell the righteous for silver, and the poor for a pair of sandals. They pant after the dust of the earth which is on the head of the poor, and pervert the way of the humble" (6,7). The law of the LORD specifically required Israel to take care of the poor and needy, but they had adopted the world's attitude of indifference toward those in need. Those who should have received special care by those in authority take the brunt of their selfish and unjust behaviour.

Neglect of the people God had placed in their care was often a deliberate act. Human needs were compromised, and in some cases ignored altogether, as the people of the Northern kingdom fed their obsession with possessions, riches and pleasure. The accumulation of wealth meant more to them than the well-being of a fellow covenant child. They were willing to take bribes, cheat and do whatever it took to get what they wanted.

Furthermore, there was no justice for the poor because the rich ran the court system. Whoever appealed for justice found it was denied them. The judges who were called to see that justice was done accepted bribes and condemned innocent people. This is what is meant by "selling the righteous for silver."

When the LORD freed His people from the bondage and slavery of Egypt He gave them specific guidelines as to how they were to protect the poor and needy. For example, we read in Exodus 23:6, "You shall not pervert the judgment of your poor in his dispute." Israel was supposed to champion the cause of the poor (Deut 15:7-11). It was the duty of kings and of the religious leaders to protect and provide for the needy (see Psalm 72). Instead both leaders and people followed the practices of heathen cultures and made money off the backs of the poor. They oppressed them and left them vulnerable and defenceless. The needy were mistreated if they could not repay a debt for which a pair of sandals had been given in pledge.

Not every Israelite was guilty of engaging in practices that brought harm upon fellow believers. Yet the people as a whole were guilty of trampling the poor and pushing them out of the way. They did not consider the needs of others. They allowed others to cheat and oppress the poor because it would not be to their advantage to say something about it. Many were blind to the needs of those who crossed their paths daily.

In verse 8 Amos also condemns those who took garments in pledge. This refers to a common practice of giving a loan and accepting the debtor's outer cloak as security for the loan. In some cases such a practice was acceptable. There were other situations, however, in which the practice was illegal.

Specifically, the law prohibited taking a poor person's garment overnight. Moreover, an Israelite was not allowed to take such a garment from a poor or needy individual. In Deut 24:12,13,17 we read, "And if the man is poor, you shall not keep his pledge overnight. You shall in any case return the pledge to him again when the sun goes down, that he may sleep in his own garment and bless you; and it shall be righteousness to you before the LORD your God... You shall not pervert justice due the stranger or the father- less, nor take a widow's garment as a pledge." But the Northern kingdom of Israel rejected what the LORD said and hardened their hearts against their brothers and sisters. Without any qualms they took the garments of the needy and made a bed for themselves out of it. They reclined, indulging in sexual sin, upon the very garments they had taken from the people they oppressed.

The Northern kingdom of Israel neglected the standard of being set apart and of living as God's holy people. The LORD will not hold them guiltless but will punish them for it. They were no different from their heathen neighbours as they looked only to themselves.

They were self-serving and intent on gaining their own profit.

The book of Deuteronomy gives specific direction as to how the people of the LORD were to show compassion to the afflicted by providing for their needs. The fatherless and widows were not left to fend for themselves; nor were they sent to some cold, impersonal government agency such as welfare or social assistance. The people of the covenant were instructed to practice religion by making sure the fatherless, widows and orphans were included in the religious festivals and the occasions in which the covenant community celebrated the goodness and mercy of the LORD. The church is to reflect God's tender care and compassion by caring for the orphans and widows (Deut, 10:18; 14:28,29; 26:12; 27:19).

Amos' preaching against the injustices of his day had as background the covenant law of the LORD. Whereas many looked to fill their own pocket, God's law made righteousness and love for one's neighbour a top priority.

The same holds true today. Certainly, we would not trample the heads of the poor into the dust! We care for the poor and the needy. We put money in the collection bag (plate) every week. Nevertheless, the Word of the LORD requires that we all search our hearts and examine our budgets. Compare the percentage of our resources that are used for our own well-being, comfort and pleasure with the amount that goes out to the needs of others both within and outside our own community.

As a child of the LORD, who has the mind of Christ, you are to seek the protection, provision and care of those who are in need. When you help a widow or person in need, you should not be preying on their vulnerability or trying to get something out of it for yourself but those being helped should see in you a genuine desire to assist – a desire which is motivated by your love for the LORD.

The fact that you have been set apart as a holy people ought to be seen in your business dealings and everything that involves the use of money. Let Christian businessmen and labourers stand out as being honest and trustworthy, as those who go to work with the care of God's people at heart.

DESPISING GOD'S STANDARD FOR MARRIAGE

Five out of the seven charges against the Northern kingdom involve economic and social affairs. The two remaining charges involve issues of morality and sexual chastity. Amos shows the people how the wrath of the LORD will come upon them because moral absolutes have fallen to the wayside. Israel's morals and ethics are sad news. What God had designed for marriage has become completely twisted and perverted. A father and son have sexual intercourse with the same girl, and the LORD's holy name is profaned. As in our times, people worshipped sexuality. To help let go of all restraint, wine entered the picture.

The lifestyle of the Northern kingdom was vile. The Israelites were so pleased with their sinful lifestyle that they toasted their perversity with the wine they acquired dishonestly through their corrupt legal system. God's standard for a healthy home life and for healthy intimate relationships had broken down completely.

The people of the Northern kingdom had allowed pagan practices to erode the distinctive norms of God's covenant. Sexual gratification instead of divine revelation became the driving force of life.

Today, many are afraid to say anything against the perversity of homosexuality, premarital relations, and extramarital affairs both outside and within the community of the church because the issues are too sensitive. The corruption in society affects us too. The lifestyles portrayed on soap operas, talk shows and movies become the norm. The lyrics of many forms of modern music – which are often filled with perverse sexual connotations – go right by us because we like what we hear! We like the rhythm and the beat. Do you think Satan in all his attempts to make us blend in will give us music that sounds repulsive? The lifestyle of the world will only *become* repulsive when our hearts are filled with the Holy Spirit.

It is important that we take heed to what the Holy Spirit reveals to us! When members of the church refuse to stand up for holiness, godliness and purity in their home lives, in their social relationships, they become indistinguishable from unbelievers.

Our Christian service should not degenerate into a superficial lip service. Instead we are to maintain our love for the Word of the LORD and respect what He has to say to us.

Let us be careful to stay on the path of Holy Scripture in questions of morality and sexual purity. May we concentrate on what is pure, holy and lovely. "Pure and undefiled religion before God and the Father is this: to visit orphans and widows in their trouble, and to keep oneself unspotted from the world"(James 1:27).

ISRAEL'S CONTEMPT FOR GOD'S COVENANT OF GRACE

Amos spoke the Word of the LORD in a time of great prosperity. The economy was booming and the country was on a political high. Spiritually, however, the nation of Israel had hit rock bottom. Not only did the Israelites disregard the Word of the LORD, but they also showed contempt for the grace of the LORD. Through Amos the LORD says, "Yet it was I who destroyed the Amorite before them, whose height was like the height of the cedars, and he was as strong as the oaks; yet I destroyed his fruit above, and his roots beneath. Also it was I who brought you up from the land of Egypt, and led you forty years through the wilderness, to possess the land of the Amorite. I raised up some of your sons as prophets and some of your young men as Nazirites. Is it not so, O you children of Israel?..."(verses 9-11).

You hear in these words how the LORD is grieved by the actions of His people! He is deeply hurt and disappointed to see that those who received so much have contempt for His grace. Notice the repetition of the word "I." Reminding the people how He had favoured them with His love, compassion and mercy, the LORD deliberately uses the word "I" four times.

Israel's past was a record of how the LORD had been good to His people. The LORD drove out the Amorites and other Canaanite nations before them. He was not afraid of the strength of giants. God eradicated the nations so that Israel might enjoy living in a land flowing with milk and honey. God's people received the land of Canaan as a gift of grace. This was the LORD'S crown upon the wonder of deliverance. He set them free from the slavery of Egypt and gave them a land from which they could await complete redemption and salvation in Jesus Christ.

The LORD brought down the Amorites because their sins had reached full measure (Gen 15:16). Their judgment is expressed in verse 9 in terms of root and fruit. Through what happened to the Amorites, the people of God are warned to seek the source of their life in the LORD and to stay in step with the Spirit by bringing forth good fruit (John 15:1-8; Gal 5:22-25). The axe is lying at the root of every tree that does not bear good fruit (Matt 3:10).

In verse 10 the LORD continues to review His gracious dealings with His people. While Israel was in the wilderness the eye of the LORD was upon His people. He did not leave them to fend for themselves. In all their afflictions He sought their good. For forty years they experienced pain and setbacks. The LORD tested them to purify and prepare them for entrance into the inheritance. The care of the LORD was also evident in that He gave them the necessary tools so that they could serve Him. He gave them a book outlining how they should live and He gave them prophets to explain and teach His will. God sent men to them to speak out against evil and to proclaim the glorious deeds of the LORD.

Both the prophets and the Nazirites reminded the people of their special identity as God's holy and separate people. The prophets spoke in the name of the LORD and the Nazirites' whole life was consecrated to the LORD. The Nazirites were to make visible the humility of heart and purity of conduct the LORD requires of His children.

From the beginning of their life as a nation, the LORD demonstrated His love and care for His people. The prophets revealed what the LORD required by their words and the Nazirites did so by their actions and example. He let the heathen nations continue in their sinful ways but the eye of His love was always upon them.

The LORD had shown Himself faithful in establishing His covenant, as promised to Abraham, and in raising up prophets to teach His will to the people. But Israel showed contempt for the undeserved favour the LORD had shown them. They tried to prevent the prophets and the Nazirites from being what they were called to be. They made the Nazirites drink wine and they commanded the prophets: "You shall not prophesy."

The worst thing that can happen to us is to become deaf to the Word of the LORD and to show contempt for the grace He has shown us in Christ. We will become blind to our own sinfulness and we will ultimately come under the heavy wrath of God. He will not hold us guiltless for our unbelief.

In the office of all believers we are called to be prophets and in our Christian conduct we are to be New Testament Nazirites, that is, we are to be a people consecrated to the LORD. May it be the prayer of all of us, "Take my life and let it be consecrated, LORD to thee. Take my moments and my days; let them flow in endless praise." Acknowledging the LORD's grace means bringing forth fruits of thankfulness wherever we may be and in all we do. Let there be growing evidence that God has called us to bask in the marvellous light of His Word. Rather than letting our lives blend in with the world around us, let us blend in a song of thanksgiving for God's grace in Christ.

Questions

1. Of what sin are the people of Judah guilty (2:4,5)? Is their sin more heinous than the transgression of Israel?

2. What is the meaning of what we find in verse six, "Because they sell the righteous for silver, and the poor for a pair of sandals?" Is such a phrase applicable to our own times?

3. What does the LORD require of a husband and wife in marriage? Look up Ephesians 5:22-33, 1 Thessalonians 4:3-8, Hebrews 13:4 and 1 Peter 3:1-7. In what ways do we show a lack of respect for God's standard for marriage?

4. How can we keep ourselves unstained from the world? In your answer consider the implications of such passages as Psalm 101, Philippians 4:8 and 1 John 2:17. Why might it be a good idea to put such texts in places where we are tempted such as the TV, VCR or computer?

5. What forms for discussion could we make use of within the communion of saints to help keep ourselves and our children

from the danger of world conformity?

6. What does chapter 2:9-11 tell us about the LORD's relationship with His people?

7. Who were the Nazirites (see Numbers 6:1-21)? How were
they to consecrate themselves to the LORD?

8. Verse 12 tells us how the people of Israel tried to silence the
voice of true prophecy. In which way does that happen
within the church today?

CHAPTER 4

DEFENDING THE TRUTH OF GOD'S WORD

Reading: Deuteronomy 7:1-13
Song selection: Psalms 33, 50,106,147

Key verses: Amos 3:1-8
Hear this word that the LORD has spoken against you, O children of Israel, against the whole family which I brought up from the land of Egypt, saying:
"You only have I known of all the families of the earth; Therefore I will punish you for all your iniquities."

Can two walk together, unless they are agreed?
Will a lion roar in the forest, when he has no prey?
Will a young lion cry out of his den, if he has caught nothing?
Will a bird fall into a snare on the earth, where there is no trap for it?
Will a snare spring up from the earth, if it has caught nothing at all?
If a trumpet is blown in a city, will not the people be

afraid?
If there is calamity in a city, will not the LORD *have done it?*

Surely the LORD *God does nothing,*
Unless He reveals His secret to His servants the prophets.
A lion has roared!
Who will not fear?
The LORD *God has spoken!*
Who can but prophesy?

*T*he book of Amos is a collection of sermons preached against the Northern kingdom of Israel during the reign of Jeroboam II. The first sermon contains a pattern of punishment and judgment that started with the nations furthest removed from Israel and then moved to the centre of the nations: to the church of the living God. Eight times we heard the phrase, "Thus says the LORD: 'For three transgressions of ... and for four, I will not turn away its ...'" The LORD tells one nation after another how He will punish their sin and transgression.

The fury of God's wrath does not stop at the door of God's covenant people. Both Israel and Judah are warned. The LORD will punish Judah because she rejected His law and did not keep His statutes. Rather than heeding the LORD's call to "be holy, for I the LORD your God am holy" (Leviticus 19:2), the Northern kingdom of Israel was content to blend in with the pagan nations around them.

The people of the covenant have rejected God's law, negated His salvation and forfeited God's grace because of their unbelief. They do not humble themselves before the LORD or repent of their sins. The Israelites cast the words of warning behind them (Psalm 50:17). They are not interested in listening to someone who proclaims a message of punishment and destruction. They don't mind when other people are condemned, but they find it hard to accept when the prophet points the finger at them.

ISRAEL'S POSITION IS SPECIAL

The prophet Amos will not be deterred or pushed around by what the people may say or think. Thus in chapter 3:1-8 he clarifies why he must continue preaching. His voice cannot be stopped.

In the first two verses of Amos 3 the prophet defends why he must speak the truth of God's Word. He puts us in touch with a theme that we find throughout Scripture. For one of the great descriptions of the church of both Old and New Dispensation can be summed up with what the LORD says through Amos in verse 2, "You only have I known of all the families of the earth." The covenant people are the chosen people of God.

These verses highlight several issues. First of all, even though the Northern kingdom of Israel has gone its separate way both politically and economically, this did not give them the right to go one step further and separate themselves from Judah in matters of faith and obedience. The LORD called and chose the twelve tribes of Israel to be His special people. He rescued them from bondage and at Mount Sinai confirmed and established His covenant with them. What God had joined together, the Northern kingdom of Israel had no right to break apart.

The citizens of the Northern kingdom are part of the whole family of God's people, and that is why they must hear the words their covenant God speaks against them, "Hear this word that the LORD has spoken against you, O children of Israel, against the whole family which I brought up from the land of Egypt."

Secondly, what the LORD says in verses 1 & 2 reminds the Israelites of the special relationship they have with God; they are the recipients of His electing love. "You only have I known of all the families of the earth," that is, "I lived with you in the most intimate way. When you cried out to me in anguish I paid attention to your plight. I rescued you and redeemed you from the slavery of Egypt. I did not close my ears to your cries of distress or ignore you when you were hurting. I heard your groaning. I remembered the covenant that I made with Abraham, Isaac and Jacob. I saw you and I knew your condition" (see Exodus 2:23-25). The LORD, in unmatched love, mercy and grace, blessed His chosen nation with salvation (Psalm 33).

The indications of God's special care for His people did not end once He rescued them from the tyranny of Egypt. His eye was always upon them because His ultimate purpose was to grant them complete redemption and salvation in Christ, to free them from the oppression and curse of sin. This is why the LORD carried them through the wilderness, just as someone carries a child (Deut 1:31).

Before the Israelites entered into the promised land of Canaan, Moses reminded them of the special position God had given to them. We read in Deuteronomy 7:6-8: "For you are a holy people to the LORD your God; the LORD your God has chosen you to be a people for Himself, a special treasure above all the peoples on the face of the earth. The LORD did not set His love on you nor choose you because you were more in number than any other people, for you were the least of all peoples; but because the LORD loves you, and because He would keep the oath which He swore to your fathers, the LORD has brought you out with a mighty hand, and redeemed you from the house of bondage, from the hand of Pharaoh king of Egypt." No other nation or people received such a powerful revelation or could lay hold of such a glorious claim: "You only." In covenant loyalty the LORD upheld this claim when the relationship was threatened by the enemies of God's people.

"You only" summarizes all the privileges and the blessings Israel received as those chosen by God. For centuries, Israel had been the object of God's covenant love.

Such love is made possible through the ministry of our Lord and Saviour, Jesus Christ. This is why God's care for His church does not end with the coming of the Messiah. He addresses us as the New Testament Israel saying, "But you are a chosen generation, a royal priesthood, a holy nation, His own special people..." (1 Peter 2:9). Through Christ He continues to separate for Himself a church chosen to everlasting life. God's grace allows us to be part of His chosen people.

Every text of Scripture which speaks of the special position of God's people stresses that the act of choosing always originates with the LORD and is rooted in His sovereign and amazing grace. At the same time, Scripture also indicates that a response is expected from those who are chosen. Take as an example what we read in Deuteronomy 7:11. After outlining their special position, God warns Israel,"Therefore you shall keep the commandment, the statutes, and the judgments, which I command you today, to observe them." We are chosen in Christ that we should be holy and blameless before Him (Ephesians 1:4).

In the covenant every privilege comes with a responsibility; every promise includes an obligation. No one who hears the gospel, who belongs to the assembly of God's people, can shrug this off and say, "Why should I care how I live? I cannot do anything about my election anyway." Having been placed by God in the covenant of grace, we are called and obliged to a new obedience.

This is exactly where Israel went wrong! They were aware of the grace of the LORD in electing and choosing them, but they did not heed their covenant obligations. They used their position as an excuse and a license to sin. They argued, "We have wealth and prosperity now, so why not enjoy life? Obviously the LORD is blessing us! If business is booming why be negative and say, 'The economic forecast doesn't look too good. This cannot last.'"

Amos' contemporaries believed God's choosing excluded the possibility of judgment, deportation or exile. They were convinced the LORD would continue to say: "You only have I known of all the families of the earth; therefore I will *redeem* you of all your iniquities." It did not occur to the people of the Northern kingdom that God's punishment might come upon them; therefore, they did not appreciate Amos' criticism. They did, however, long for the day of the LORD when He would come to judge the nations.

The people of God feel at ease and are convinced nothing ill will happen to them because they are blind to their own sin. They do not understand what it means to live in the covenant of grace. They do not know the LORD or live in close communion with Him. The covenant people are careless and show contempt for the grace of the LORD. It doesn't bother them to blend in with the world around them or to worship the LORD according to their own wishes and preferences.

To counter such thinking, Amos, on the LORD's behalf, has some shocking news to tell. "You only have I known of all the families of the earth; therefore I will *punish* you for all your iniquities." The covenant relationship will testify against them if they do not repent from their sins. Israel must live as a redeemed people whose only hope and consolation is salvation, forgiveness and renewal in Christ.

Amos exhorts Israel to heed what the LORD is saying to them precisely because of the special position they have been given in God's sovereign grace and mercy. He proclaims in chapter 5:18, 20,"Woe to you who desire the day of the LORD! For what good is the day of the LORD to you? It will be darkness, and not light. Is not the day of the LORD darkness, and not light? Is it not very dark, with no brightness in it?" And in chapter 6:1 he warns, "Woe to you who are at ease in Zion, and trust Mount Samaria, notable persons in the chief nation, to whom the house of Israel comes!"

We, as children of God, are fooling ourselves if we think the LORD will not judge us for our actions because we belong to the covenant people of the LORD. It is true that the LORD has chosen to redeem us. But the covenant relationship consists of promises and demands. We are saved in Christ to serve the LORD as His thankful, loyal and obedient children. Those who have been called must work *out* what God is working *in* them (Phil. 2:12,13). Those who have been promised freedom from the slavery of sin must live like free people.

In the community of God's people we feel safe living in God's grace, but such security is only truly ours when we flee to the crucified Christ and take refuge in Him. True peace comes only through faith, that is, through an obedient response to both the promises and the demands of God's covenant. Let us, therefore, encourage one another to stand in awe of God's grace *and* to walk by faith, all the more as we see the Day drawing near (Hebrews 10:24,25).

ISRAEL'S REASONING IS FAULTY

The prophet Amos also demonstrates that Israel must hear the truth of God's words because their reasoning is faulty. By asking several rhetorical questions, Amos illustrates how it would be unnatural and irresponsible if he would remain silent. Contrary to their demands, he cannot keep quiet when the LORD commands him to prophesy.

In verses 3-5 Amos describes several scenarios from human relationships and from the natural world of animals in which he tries to show Israel that their reasoning is faulty.

The first involves a relationship between two individuals who have agreed to walk together: "Can two walk together, unless they are agreed?" Travelling through the Palestinian countryside was often hazardous. Some parts were too dangerous to go alone. Thus if two agreed to travel together, they would trust that the one would not leave the other. The two were bound to each other by mutual agreement. If two people are seen walking together it can be assumed that they have agreed to do so.

Amos also provides a number of examples from the animal kingdom. "Will a lion roar in the forest, when he has no prey? Will a young lion cry out of his den, if he has caught nothing? Will a bird fall into a snare on the earth, where there is no trap for it? Will a snare spring up from the earth, if it has caught nothing at all?" If a young lion is heard crying out, it should be clear that he has captured some prey. If a trap is sprung, one may conclude that an animal or a bird has wandered into it.

In a world of uncertainty, change, and unpredictability, certain natural laws will always hold true. Amos underscores another "natural law" which must be observed: a prophet who has received God's Word *must* speak that Word! Just as the Lord met with His people when they walked through the wilderness, so the Lord approaches His faithful servants and discloses to them His revelation.

The same "natural law" (or principle) holds true today. Every preacher is to sound the alarm of impending doom and destruction. If a minister preaches on a text of Scripture, he must say what the text says. If the text speaks of grace, he must preach grace. If the text speaks of sin and punishment, he must preach that too. Failure to do so would be a loveless act.

This, however, is not the end of the matter. Amos also indicates that to keep silent would be irresponsible. In verses 6-7 Amos states it this way, "If a trumpet is blown in a city, will not the people be afraid? If there is calamity in a city, will not the Lord have done it? Surely the Lord God does nothing, unless He reveals His secret to His servants the prophets."

Israel is the city of verse 6. The LORD is preparing disaster to come upon it. Amos, as a faithful prophet of the LORD, must sound the trumpet warning of impending judgment and trouble. Nevertheless, there is still hope for Israel! The LORD *allows* Amos to sound the alarm. There is still time for repentance.

A prophet would act irresponsibly if he refused to proclaim the message which the LORD revealed to him. Do you see how the LORD in His compassion seeks Israel's repentance? He sends Amos to Israel so that his preaching would cause them to tremble in holy fear before God's greatness.

On the LORD's behalf, Amos asks a number of rhetorical questions to show his audience how serious their predicament has become. If they do not heed the Word of the LORD, but continue to laugh it off, they will feel the truth of the words that have been spoken. What they have received in the covenant will be taken from them.

ISRAEL'S PREDICAMENT IS SERIOUS

In verse 8 Amos puts himself in the line of fire, reminding his hearers that he too would be worthy of judgment if he kept the prophetic message to himself. "A lion has roared! Who will not fear? The LORD God has spoken! Who can but prophesy?" The prophet does not speak on his own authority. He does not come with his own suggestions for change. The LORD has spoken; therefore, Amos has no choice but to speak.

Every Israelite shepherd and farmer knew how the roar of the lion could break the peace of a quiet evening. The sheep would huddle nervously together and it would strike fear into the heart of the bravest shepherd. Both man and animal knew what the lion's roar meant. When the shepherd heard the roar of the lion he did not debate, "Shall I be afraid or not?" His heart would race and he would do everything to defend his sheep.

Thus Amos, speaking the truth in love for the sheep of God's pasture, warns them that they are in danger. If Amos had kept silent he would have been disloyal to his master and would have shown a lack of care for the sheep. Refusing to prophesy would be as foolish and as dangerous as refusing to heed the angry roar of a lion. But the prophet is a faithful servant of his Master (3:7). He is God's spokesman, announcing the LORD's will to His people.

Presently, the LORD in His mercy reveals His secret counsel and will concerning the judgment and punishment that will come upon those who do not honour and serve the LORD. The LORD is still gracious. If there is no repentance, there will come a time when the Word of the LORD will be taken away from them. As we read in chapter 8:11, 12, "Behold, the days are coming," says the LORD God, "that I will send a famine on the land, not a famine of bread, nor a thirst for water, but of hearing the words of the LORD. They shall wander from sea to sea, and from north to east; they shall run to and fro, seeking the word of the LORD, but shall not find it." The light of the gospel and the privileges of the covenant will be taken away from those who live in disobedience. The lampstand of God's Word will be removed. That can happen to individuals, but also to whole church communities.

The secret counsel and will of God concerning our redemption has been fully revealed to us by our chief prophet and teacher, Jesus Christ. God's covenant grace and mercy have been made known to us through the ministry of our Saviour. His conception, birth, ministry, suffering, death, resurrection and ascension all speak of the glorious freedom we have received. Let us never take for granted our special position as members of Jesus Christ. May it be our sincere desire to serve the LORD in covenant obedience so that we may continue to hear proclaimed to us, "You only have I known of all the families of the earth; therefore I will forgive you all your sins and heal all your iniquities."

Questions

1. What is the significance of the wording, "the LORD has spoken against you, O children of Israel, against the whole family which I brought up from the land of Egypt" (3:1)? Does this verse have any bearing on how we speak about churches which have deviated from the Word of the LORD?

2. What is the meaning of the phrase, "You only have I known of all the families of the earth?" Compare chapter 3:2 with Deut 7 and Psalm 147. How do these passages help us understand the relationship between covenant and election?

3. Chapter 3:6 says: "If there is calamity in a city, will not the LORD have done it?" How is this to be explained in view of our confession "God is not the author of sin" (Belgic Confession Article 13 and Canons of Dort Chapter I, Article 15)?

4. In chapter 3:7 we read, "Surely the LORD God does nothing, unless He reveals His secret to His servants the prophets." Why does the LORD alert His prophets about what He is planning to do?

5. How are we to respond to the preaching of God's Word? Look up passages of Scripture that show the power of preaching (e.g. Isaiah 52:7; Romans 10:8-17; 1 Corinthians 2:1-5; Hebrews 4:11-13).

6. Why do covenant people who receive God's blessing still need to hear words of warning and judgment?

7. In His mercy the LORD reveals to us our covenant obligations. Give examples of these obligations from both the Old and New Testament.

8. How can a minister/congregation know if the whole counsel of God is being preached?

9. Give New Testament examples of how the Word of the LORD can be taken away from a people who walk in disobedience. What images does the LORD use to describe how He will take away from His people the riches they have received in Christ?

CHAPTER 5

THE WORD OF THE LORD TO DISOBEDIENT COVENANT WOMEN

Reading: Proverbs 31:10-31; Isaiah 3:13-4:6; Amos 3:9-14
Song selection: Psalms 48, 113, 128

Key verses: Amos 4:1-3
Hear this word, you cows of Bashan, who are on the mountain of Samaria,
Who oppress the poor,
Who crush the needy,
Who say to your husbands, "Bring wine, let us drink!"
The LORD God has sworn by His holiness:
"Behold, the days shall come upon you
When He will take you away with fishhooks,
And your posterity with fishhooks.
You will go out through broken walls,
Each one straight ahead of her,
And you will be cast into Harmon,"
Says the LORD.

*B*oth within the home and the church, women have a tremen-dous influence – either for good or for evil. Women can stand in the service of the LORD or be instruments of the devil. Many men have been helped by women and many men have been seduced and led down a wrong path by women. Indeed, women play a very important role in the spiritual stability of family life and within the communion of saints.

The Bible gives numerous examples of women who were the backbone of the men in the church. It speaks of women of faith who actively sought to further Christ's kingdom through their humble and faithful service. Women who were alone or widowed served an important function in the spread of the gospel by assisting the needs of prophets, apostles and ministers of the Word. Think of the women who helped Elijah, Elisha and the apostle Paul.

Whether we care to admit it or not, it is no exaggeration to say that the deeds of many men have been determined and can be explained by the women in their lives. But that influence is not always positive.

When churches do not worship the LORD according to His Word, the order and structure the LORD designed falls apart and is turned upside down. Children and teenagers start "calling the shots" and parents are too afraid to speak out against it. Women take upon themselves a role that does not belong to them because men are not giving proper leadership in the home or in church life.

Every church member is duty-bound to worship the LORD in obedience to His Word. Men in the church have a tremendous task to show themselves to be godly and faithful leaders. But they do not stand alone. For the church consists of brothers and sisters in Christ who stand beside each other and work together as fellow heirs of grace! Men may not go their own way and neither may women.

In this passage we are told how the LORD punishes those women who do not serve the well-being of the whole church but who have become selfish, proud, arrogant and whose thinking is focussed on the needs of the flesh.

WHAT HE HAS AGAINST THESE WOMEN

The prophet doesn't come with anything new in chapter 4:1-3. Amos narrows his focus to confirm what he stated in chapter 3:9-15. The people of God have become self-seeking and self-indulgent. Selfishness is rampant. The life of the people is organized around one guiding principle: what is in it for me. This is the picture the women of Samaria portray as well.

Amos condemns the sinful attitude of women in the covenant who consider themselves religious and God-fearing but who, with haughty pride, push their own way both in family life and in the church. Just as Eve in Paradise led Adam down the "garden path," so the women of Samaria lead their husbands down the crooked road of disobedience. The costs and consequences are tremendous. The women of Samaria do not care what happens to others. It doesn't bother them that the poor are oppressed and the needy are crushed. As long as they get their way they are happy. These women spend their waking hours on matters pertaining to the body rather than focussing on their own spiritual well-being, that of their families, and of the whole church.

The influence of the women of the Northern kingdom – represented by the capital, Samaria – is evil and corrupt. Amos says, "Hear this word, you cows of Bashan!" To be called a cow wouldn't have been exactly complimentary or flattering, to say the least. It's not hard to imagine how women would react if a minister said, "Hear this, you women of the church, you herd of fat cows – well fed, sleek and lazy." They wouldn't take to that very kindly. Today we may smile about it, but the women in the Northern kingdom of Israel would have been upset. How does this farmer from Tekoa dare to call them "cows of Bashan"?

No one accepts criticism easily, especially when it involves matters of lifestyle. It's a touchy subject. So why wasn't the prophet more gentle in his approach? Could he not have used more tact?

Amos stood before these women as a messenger of the LORD of hosts. The prophet is not going out of his way to be rude, derogatory or impolite. He speaks the Word of the LORD in language that is meant to drive home a point. The Word of the LORD can be very straightforward.

The women of Samaria do not serve the cause of Christ and they must be made aware of it for their own good and for the holiness of the covenant people. What the LORD says to the women of Samaria affects everybody, including the men and children. These women belong to the people to whom the LORD has said, "You only have I known of all the families of the earth" (3:2), and they are in danger of forfeiting the riches of the covenant. Amos compares them to the cows of *Bashan* because Bashan was known for its well-fed cattle.

Amos levels three charges against the women of Israel. First, they encourage the oppression of the poor. Secondly, they crush the needy. The third charge is more subtle, but it gets right down to the "nitty gritty" of what exactly is going on. Quoting their own words Amos accuses them of a self-centred lifestyle. They say to their husbands, "Bring wine, let us drink!" These women may not directly cheat the poor in the marketplace nor deny them justice in the courts. Nevertheless, they are held responsible for the condition in which the covenant people find themselves. Their part in the oppression of the powerless consists of putting demands on their husbands to maintain a highly expensive lifestyle. The women of Samaria have their husbands at their beck and call to feed their own secular lifestyle! They have made their husbands into slaves.

As was mentioned before, the Northern kingdom of Israel enjoyed a time of exceptional prosperity during the reign of Jeroboam II. Especially those who lived in cities such as Samaria enjoyed immense luxury. Revelling in this, women demanded of their husbands that their liquor cabinets be kept full and enough money be made to support a high-class style of living. These women are so preoccupied with their own things and absorbed in the pursuit of luxury that they are blind to the needs of others and their husbands let them get away with it! The men show no leadership and therefore there is no love or concern for fellow brothers and sisters. They ignore what the LORD wrote in Proverbs 14:21 and 31, "He who despises his neighbour sins; but he who has mercy on the poor, happy is he...He who oppresses the poor reproaches his Maker, but he who honours Him has mercy on the needy."

A woman who knows her rightful place within the church of

Christ is able to stretch a dollar for the sake of God's kingdom. She is wise and discerning and will not have a huge list of demands that feed her own pleasures. In Amos 4 we are given a sad picture of selfishness and apostasy. The behaviour of the men was already bad enough. A son and his father go into the same maiden thereby profaning the name of the LORD. But the women were no better. They did not live in holiness or modesty nor did they serve the coming of Christ's kingdom. Their portrait did not match that of the woman of faith as described in Proverbs 31.

According to Proverbs 31 a woman of faith opens her mouth with wisdom, and the law (instruction) of kindness is on her tongue. She opens her hand to the poor, looks to the ways of her household, and does not eat the bread of idleness. She is constantly busy with the task the LORD has given to her. Consequently, her children rise up and call her blessed; her husband also, and he praises her! Proverbs 31 shows there is nothing praiseworthy about a woman who separates herself from her God-given task and concentrates on material gain and outward adornment. "Charm is deceitful and beauty is passing, But a woman who fears the LORD, she shall be praised." A woman of faith exhibits the inner beauty of a heart set on God's service.

The women of Samaria are sleek and well-groomed like the cows that came from Bashan. The district of Bashan was a large region across the Jordan River which was known for its large cattle herds and rich pastureland. The cows that came from this region were fed well and prized highly. This is the kind of environment in which the women of Samaria lived. They had everything they needed. Yet they were not satisfied. The more they received the more they demanded; they could not satisfy their enormous appetite for luxury.

No matter what the issue may be, if women in the covenant start demanding that they get their way rather than unselfishly serving the well-being of others it will not go well with the whole congregation. A husband has the responsibility to provide for his family. He may not spend his money on his own pleasures and neither may his wife. A woman should not become so demanding that there is no money to support those in need. When men, women or children break the order the LORD established God will not let it go unpunished. The same is true here. The LORD will punish these women by sending them away into exile.

As God's adopted children we deserve nothing of what we have received from the hand of the LORD. Therefore both men and women in the church should allow every aspect of their life to come under the scrutiny of God's Holy Word. We have to train ourselves to accept and work with criticism even if what the LORD says may hurt us! The LORD wants us to hear His criticism for our good so that we should turn our hearts to Him and to His Son Jesus Christ. He disciplines us so that we should seek after the holiness without which no one will see the LORD. For the moment all discipline seems painful rather than pleasant; later it yields the peaceful fruit of righteousness to those who have been trained by it (Hebrews 12:11,14).

WHAT HE SAYS AGAINST THESE WOMEN
In verses 2 & 3 Amos describes in a nutshell what the LORD will do. "The LORD God has sworn by His holiness: 'Behold the days shall come upon you when He will take you away with fishhooks, and your posterity with fishhooks.'" This is not the first time the LORD swore by His holiness. He swore to Abraham, Isaac and Jacob, promising under oath to give His people all they needed. On more than one occasion the LORD swore to underline and confirm that He can be trusted. He does not *need* to swear because all His words and all His promises are reliable, faithful and trustworthy. There is no greater guarantor of covenant reliability and faithfulness (Hebrews 6:13). The LORD will always be faithful to his covenant, both in blessing and punishment.

As the people of Israel were about to enter Canaan, the LORD, in covenant faithfulness, promised to bless them. He swore with an oath to take care of all their needs. We read in Deuteronomy 28:7-9,11, "The LORD will cause your enemies who rise against you to be defeated before your face; they shall come out against you one way and flee before you seven ways. The LORD will command the blessing on you in your storehouses and in all to which you set your hand, and He will bless you in the land which the LORD your God is giving you. The LORD will establish you as a holy people to Himself, just as He has sworn to you, if you keep the command-ments of the LORD your God and walk in His ways...And the LORD will grant you plenty of goods, in the fruit of your body, in the increase of your livestock, and in the produce of your ground, in the land of which the LORD swore to your fathers to give you."

The LORD may never be accused of being stingy or negligent. He consistently promises to provide His people with all that they need for body and soul. He lets us enjoy the riches of being His covenant children. Yet we are called to be good stewards of God's blessings. What we receive has been given to us *within* the commu-nion of the LORD's people and *for* communion with the LORD's people.

But the people of the Northern kingdom of Israel – and in particular the women – do not make good use of what the LORD has granted to them in His grace. The women of Samaria are richly supplied with all they need; yet, like stubborn heifers they kick and resist the LORD's guidance. Deuteronomy 32:15 gives a fitting description, "But Jeshurun grew fat and kicked; you grew fat, you grew thick, you are obese! Then he forsook God who made him, and scornfully esteemed the Rock of his salvation." They kick against God's law and don't want the prophets to remind them of their sin. The land of rest becomes a land of sleep. They do not have an open eye for God's faithfulness and love.

The women who were first addressed as cows are also described as fish who are dragged along with a hook. Just as fish are caught and dragged out of their natural environment, these women will be hooked and taken out of their comfortable places and led away into captivity. Like a fisherman who pulls a fish out of the water, so the LORD will pull the women of Samaria out of their self-indulgent and luxurious lifestyles and He will bring them into exile. They will lose everything, including all those outward things they considered to be so important! Lined up in single file like so many cattle, these women of Samaria will be led, pushed and shoved through the breaches the invaders will make in the city walls. They will begin the long trek to the land of exile.

This is not the only time the LORD judges the negative influence of women in the church. We read another example of it in Isaiah 3. There, too, the women are pictured as being haughty, proud and above criticism. They are full of themselves but not of the service of the LORD and the effects are devastating.

The LORD had sworn in His holiness to care for His people if they would continue to walk in the ways of His covenant. He promised to provide them with all good, avert all evil or turn it to their benefit. But as the LORD lives He will also be faithful to His Word of judgment and punishment. For He had also sworn that if they did not walk in His ways they would be punished.

We, too, are warned by this passage to maintain the covenant relationship the LORD has established with us. If we become lazy and "fat" and start "kicking back" the LORD will bring us into judgment. If we use what the LORD has given us for our own pleasure and purposes He will judge us. We, who have received the grace of the LORD, are called to live for others, to serve the needs and the well-being of the flock for whom Christ shed His blood.

We live under Him who has sworn in His holiness to bless us. Keep that in mind at all times – also when it comes to your spending habits and how you use what the LORD allows you. We live in the presence of a holy God who will not turn a blind eye to our sins. If we are driven by greed rather than by the LORD's service, our life will ultimately become very empty and meaningless.

The LORD does not take it lightly when individuals neglect their responsibilities within the communion of His covenant people or when they misuse what He has entrusted to them. He will take away what we have. We will become like fish out of water – spiritually dead.

Christ is our only hope for the future. He washes away the filth of the daughters of Zion and cleanses them from the stain of sin. Jesus renews us so that we can serve Him and one another in love and holiness. Let us all together, men, women and children, listen to the voice of the LORD and respond to it in faith and obedience by gratefully fulfilling the task that is given to us. May our men be true sons of Abraham and show themselves to be men of faith and conviction. May our women be true daughters of Sarah – women of faith who adorn themselves with the imperishable jewel of a gentle and quiet spirit, which in God's sight is very precious.

Questions

1. What is meant by the expression "who store up violence and robbery" (3:10)?

2. Throughout his entire prophecy Amos speaks out against sins that are committed against fellow believers (see Amos 3:9,10). Why are sins against each other frequently downplayed?

3. Why is it particularly remarkable that Ashdod and Egypt (3:9) will sit in judgment on Israel's oppression of the poor and needy?

4. Chapter 3:12 returns to the lion theme. How is that motif used differently here than in chapter 1:2 and 3:3,4?

5. Just as a piece of an ear or two legs point to the former existence of a sheep, Israel's existence will find its remnants in a corner of a bed or the edge of a couch (3:12). What does this say about the religious state of the Northern kingdom?

6. The LORD says that He will punish Israel for their transgression and will visit destruction on the altars of Bethel. What was the significance of the horns of the altar being cut off and falling to the ground (3:14)?

7. How does verse 14 show the failure of the worship of the Northern kingdom?

8. Outline the task that is given by Scripture to men and women of faith. Why does it happen that women take on a role that does not belong to them?

9. How can women be a positive influence in the church? Give examples from both the Old and New Testament as to how this was done. What role can they have within the church today?

10. Is the woman of Proverbs 31 an ideal to follow or an example of covenant obedience? Explain the difference.

11. How can parents train their daughters to avoid imitating the image of women portrayed in secular magazines?

12. Look up those passages of Scripture which speak about God's "swearing by His holiness." What does this phrase mean? How did the self- pleasing attitude of the women of Samaria fly in the face of God's holiness?

CHAPTER 6

THE CALL TO RETURN TO TRUE WORSHIP

Reading: Deuteronomy 12:1-14; 1 Kings 12:25-33
Song selection: Psalms 27,42,84,122,135

Key verses: Amos 4:4-5; 5:4-6

"Come to Bethel and transgress,
At Gilgal multiply transgression;
Bring your sacrifices every morning,
Your tithes every three days.
Offer a sacrifice of thanksgiving with leaven,
Proclaim and announce the freewill offerings;
For this you love,
You children of Israel!"
Says the LORD *God.*

For thus says the LORD *to the house of Israel:*
"Seek Me and live;
But do not seek Bethel,
Nor enter Gilgal,

Nor pass over to Beersheba;
For Gilgal shall surely go into captivity,
And Bethel shall come to nothing.
Seek the LORD *and live,*
Lest He break out like fire in the house of Joseph.
And devour it,
With no one to quench it in Bethel -
You who turn justice to wormwood,
And lay righteousness to rest in the earth!"

When we assemble together to worship the LORD we come before Him in an active and living relationship of covenant communion. As the LORD meets with His people He reveals to us His will and His ways. We listen and respond in prayer and praise to His words of love, comfort, admonition, direction and encouragement. What we hear is meant to draw us closer to the LORD in commitment, holiness and love so that we serve Him all the days of the week with joy and devotion.

As we worship we are to recognize that we are in the presence of a holy God. Our whole manner of worship is not a matter of indifference or personal preference. We may not worship our covenant Father according to the desires of our own hearts. Everything we do is to be regulated by the principles of Holy Scripture. Where we go to church is not a matter of choice but is an act of obedience. We bend our knees in submission to Christ.

Submission to Christ and to the will of God the Father must determine how we worship Him, too. We do not come together to be entertained or to entertain. No one should be drawing attention to himself since all our attention should be on the majesty and glory of the LORD. We are drawing near to the LORD in the beauty of His holiness.

Throughout Scripture the LORD condemns all forms of worship, however pious they may seem, that do not conform with His Word and that move us away from the central truth of the gospel. Doing what we like, what makes us feel good, or puts us on an emotional high is not necessarily what God wants! The first question of worship always is: "Does this please the LORD and is it in harmony with His will? Does it honour the LORD and bring praise to His name? Does it focus on the grace of God in Christ?"

We may not always feel excited in our worship of God. That could be the result of things we have experienced during the week that interfere with our listening. It could also be that we do not fully understand the meaning of the elements of worship. For example, we may not have learned to appreciate the meaning of the psalms, the significance of the offerings or why a particular order of worship is important. Once we lose a Biblical perspective on worship we stick to what we have out of tradition or we end up drifting into a sea of changes. Worship becomes subject to the likes and dislikes of the congregation or to the dictates of those who happen to serve in office.

This was what was wrong in the Northern kingdom of Israel! The people were very faithful in going to their centres of worship and they were very religious, but they had created a church of their own making. In chapter 4:4,5 and chapter 5:4-6 the LORD speaks out against the religious practices of the day. Therefore we must listen carefully to what the Holy Spirit teaches in these passages.

THE LORD DENOUNCES WHAT THEY ARE DOING

From our previous studies in the book of Amos, we know that the prophet spoke harsh words to the people of Israel. The Israelites violated the covenant with the LORD God in nearly every imaginable way. In Amos 4:4-5 the prophet details how even their worship has become abhorrent to the LORD, " 'Come to Bethel and transgress, at Gilgal multiply transgression; bring your sacrifices every morning, your tithes every three days. Offer a sacrifice of thanksgiving with leaven, proclaim and announce the freewill offerings; for this you love, You children of Israel!' says the LORD God."

Amos' indictment is directed against three centres of worship. Amos 4 mentions the first two, Bethel and Gilgal, and Amos 5 mentions the third, Beersheba.

What exactly was Amos driving at by referring to these three: Beersheba, Bethel and Gilgal? All three places had an important function within the history of God's redemptive deeds. As you may recall, Bethel was the place where the LORD met Jacob in a dream. When Jacob awoke from the dream he said, "Surely the LORD is in this place and I did not know it." He called the place "Bethel" which means, "house of God." Bethel remained an important place in the time of the judges and when King Solomon died and the kingdom was split. One of the places Jeroboam I chose as an official centre for worship was Bethel. It became the place where the royal family worshipped and therefore it was called "the king's sanctuary" and a "temple of the kingdom" (Amos 7:13).

Gilgal was the place where the covenant was renewed under Joshua and later again under Samuel. After crossing the Jordan River, as recorded in Joshua 3 & 4, a pile of stones was set there as a memorial of what the LORD had done to bring His people into the promised land. Gilgal was also the first place in the promised land where the Passover was celebrated and it was the location where Israel made Saul king in the presence of the LORD.

Like Bethel, Gilgal had recently been elevated to a new status as a centre for pilgrimages and sacrifices. Both cities had prestigious histories. Beersheba did not fall far behind. For the most part Beersheba was under the control of the Southern Kingdom of Judah. This city also had significance in that all three patriarchs, Abraham, Isaac and Jacob, sought the guidance and direction from the LORD while staying in Beersheba.

But why did Amos condemn his audience for going to these centres of worship? The Israelites believed they were doing what the LORD expected of them. Why is the prophet so hard on them? The people of God seem to be going out of their way to be pious and to serve the LORD! After all, never before had the holy places which had been established in Bethel and Gilgal been so busy. An abundance of offerings was being made. Those who ministered at the holy places of Bethel, Gilgal and Beersheba were being looked after very well through an overdose of tithing! The people of the Northern kingdom were giving much more than they were required to give. Moreover, even though Jeroboam I had set up golden calves in Dan and Bethel to stop the people from going to the southern kingdom of Judah, the hostility was no longer there in the days of Jeroboam II. Many Israelites were willing to cross over into Judah and make a long trek and pilgrimage all the way to the southern end – to Beersheba.

The church in the Northern kingdom was vibrant and active. In light of all the "good things" the Israelites were doing, could the prophet maintain that they were sinning and transgressing the law of the LORD? How could he say, "Come to Bethel and transgress; to Gilgal and multiply transgression?" It doesn't seem fair that Amos should criticize them for bringing tithes and offerings or for implying that they are sinning. We would expect that the prophet would say, "Come to Bethel and worship the LORD, kneel down in His presence and acknowledge His holiness." Instead, Amos highlights where matters are going wrong.

The word used for "transgress" suggests Israel is like a spoiled, ungrateful child who steals from his aging parents (Proverbs 28:24). Israel's actions are comparable to the actions of a state, province, or part of a nation which rebels and does not want to be part of the country any longer (1 Kings 12:19). The worship of the Northern kingdom is tearing them away from the LORD. Any form of worship that is not in harmony with the revealed will of the LORD, any pattern of self-willed worship, is an act of revolution and rebellion.

You might be thinking that the prophet Amos is suggesting that we are sinning if we put too much weight on the place *where* we worship the LORD. But to surmise from this text that it doesn't matter where you go to church as long as you believe in the Lord Jesus would be a misinterpretation of what the LORD is saying. Amos is not condoning a "privatized" Christianity. What he condemns is a religion which is built upon human precepts, a religious fervour which may look impressive but which is lacking a solid Biblical foundation.

Although there appeared to be a revival in the Northern kingdom of Israel, it was a piety of pretense. Outwardly, what was going on at Bethel, Gilgal and Beersheba did not appear to be all that different from what was going on at Jerusalem. Many considered it to be a more meaningful and uplifting experience to go to these shrines. Nevertheless, the worship of the Northern kingdom did not meet God's approval. The LORD had not chosen Bethel, Gilgal or Beersheba as His dwelling place. He isn't to be worshipped in places designed and built on human opinion or choice.

According to the law of the LORD, Jerusalem alone was the legitimate place where the sanctuary and the covenant rituals should be celebrated! The LORD had chosen Zion to be His dwelling place. In fact, the bold decision of Jeroboam I to establish a new 'holy city' as an alternative to Jerusalem would be referred to throughout 1 and 2 Kings as "the sin of Jeroboam" (1 Kings 14:16; 2 Kings 10:29).

The author of Kings makes it clear that Jeroboam's action of establishing a new centre of religious activity was a direct violation of the law of the LORD. For the LORD had specifically prescribed in Deuteronomy 12 that His people were not to worship Him as they saw fit. As we read, "...to the place the LORD your God will choose as a dwelling for His Name – there you are to bring everything I command you: your burnt offerings and sacrifices, your tithes and special gifts, and all the choice possessions you have vowed to the LORD" (NIV).

The LORD specifically told Israel to worship Him in the place which He would choose. In contrast, listen to what we read in 1 Kings 12:32,33, "Jeroboam ordained a feast on the fifteenth day of the eighth month, like the feast that was in Judah, and offered sacrifices on the altar. So he did at Bethel, sacrificing to the calves *that he had made.* And at Bethel he installed the priests of the high places *which he had made.* So he made offerings on the altar which *he had made* at Bethel on the fifteenth day of the eighth month, in the month *which he had devised in his own heart...*"

It is our responsibility to be fully aware of the expectations that the LORD has for worship and to settle for nothing less than complete adherence to His standards. When worship degrades into a self-willed service, the LORD is robbed of His glory; there is little or no awareness of sin, and the worshipper loves to sound forth the wonderful things he or she is doing for the LORD. The same was true in the Northern kingdom. The people go to the wrong place with the wrong attitude. They do not approach the LORD with a humble and contrite heart or a broken spirit. Israel has no sense of grace or the need for forgiveness through the coming of the Messiah.

The iniquity and idolatry of God's people extends so far that they have made an idol out of the sacrificial system. Although they are very busy with making their offerings, they do not offer them with the precision the law required. Note, for example, the glaring omission in the list of offerings the people of the Northern kingdom bring to the LORD at Bethel and Gilgal. They bring thank offerings and freewill offerings but no mention is made of the sin offering.

The people boast about how they love the LORD and what they are able to give and do for His service but they have no concept of sin. They want it proclaimed and published how much they are giving so that everybody can admire their eagerness, generosity and piety! In reality, they have no sense of how sinful they are and how much they need the blood of atonement, and the sacrifice of Christ, to cover their lives before any thank offering and freewill offering will be acceptable and pleasing to God. A "feel-good" religion, which is void of a knowledge of sin and the need for Christ's redemption, is meaningless.

Israel is engaged in the rituals of worship simply out of a desire to be glorified and honoured themselves. They put on display their willingness to give of their freewill offerings. The LORD, however, condemns their practices. He will not accept their offerings and sacrifices. The LORD says, "Take away from me the noise of your songs for I will not hear the melody of your stringed instruments."

We, as people of God, are warned against the danger of using worship as a tool for corporate or personal glory. No one – not the minister in preaching, the congregation in singing and in the giving of their offerings, the musical accompanists in playing, may draw attention to themselves. If we do not give glory to the LORD what we are doing becomes a terrible noise before Him.

Every congregational member has a responsibility to react properly to the various aspects of the liturgy. The organists or pianists are not in church to give a recital but to help our human voices bring praise to the LORD. The most effective preachers are not those who are the most pleasant to listen to or who are up-to-date with news, or in tune with modern music and entertainment, but those who bring the unadulterated Word of God.

We do not worship to be seen by men, but to glorify God. The reason for our existence as church, why we put money in the collection bag, why we assist the needy, should not be that others admire us or know how much we give, but that the LORD may be glorified through the obedience of His people. In both Old and New Testament every aspect of worship is placed in the context of grace. God's grace in Christ draws us together and attracts outsiders. Worship is not the time to be honoured or entertained but a time to seek the LORD so that we may live.

THE LORD ANNOUNCES WHAT THEY SHOULD BE DOING

Amos says in chapter 5:4, "For thus says the LORD to the house of Israel: 'Seek me and live.'" The people of Israel knew this language! Repeatedly the LORD had called His people to seek Him. They heard it in the law and through the mouth of the LORD's servants, the prophets. By exhorting His people to seek Him, the LORD is instructing them to ask for guidance. The word "seek" carries with it a sense of urgency and tension. Those who seek the LORD will not rest until they have found Him, until they have set their hearts on the path of life. They realize that outside the LORD and the true worship of His Name there is no life, hope or future.

As those who seek the LORD, we may not take a single step without first asking for direction and guidance. God must approve everything we do including our patterns of worship – how and where we worship Him.

What we build will be broken down if we do not serve the LORD according to His Word. Our worship may flourish today and everything may appear to be going just fine so that some may conclude, "Surely God is with them." Yet if our worship is not legitimate, the LORD will break it down. Thus Gilgal went into exile and Bethel came to naught.

Seeking the LORD means coming to know Him and His redeeming ways in Christ. We seek the LORD by placing ourselves under God's supervision. It means going to a church where people surrender themselves to the will of the LORD in all things. In the popular Christianity of our day we are confronted with the notion that it does not matter where you worship the LORD because we all belong to the invisible body of believers anyway.

Without any qualms, Christians will leave a church because they do not find it friendly, because they don't like the style of worship, because it doesn't have the programs they want for their children or because there is not enough excitement or joy. In this way of thinking, going to church is like going out for dinner. You make the choice where you want to go and what you want from the menu. But the choice is not ours. We are called to serve the LORD in obedience in the place He has established. "Do not seek Bethel, nor enter Gilgal, nor pass over to Beersheba."

Everyone is duty-bound to join the assembly of believers wherever God has established it, where we are fed by His Word and gain a deeper knowledge of God's ways. In the church everyone must learn to live by the grace of the LORD. All members are to realize forgiveness of sins and eternal life are granted to the church through Christ alone. Adults and children, office-bearers and congregation, rich and poor, single or married are taught in the church to live out of the hand of the LORD and not to rely on their own insight.

The LORD appeals to His people to return to Him and find life in His name. Deformation can be stopped. It isn't an irreversible process. In Psalm 27, David expresses what must be the desire of every child of the LORD, "One thing I have desired of the LORD, that will I seek: that I may dwell in the house of the LORD all the days of my life, to behold the beauty of the LORD and to inquire in His temple...When you said, 'Seek my face,' my heart said to you, 'Your face, LORD, I will seek'" (4,8). In other words, we are not to seek after places of worship which please us but we are to seek to worship Him in obedience by listening to His Word, by using the sacraments, by serving the edification of brothers and sisters, according to the talents God has given us as members of the same body.

It is noteworthy that the call to worship the LORD according to His Word does not only come to the people of the Northern kingdom who have separated themselves from the worship of the LORD in Jerusalem. The LORD addresses the "house of Israel." All the covenant people of the LORD must hear what He requires of them and what they must seek after. Every one of us must seek the grace of the LORD and reconciliation through Jesus Christ – otherwise the LORD will take away what we have. This is the way verse 6 ends,

"Seek the LORD and live, lest He break out like fire in the house of Joseph, and devour it, with no one to quench it in Bethel." We are to worship the LORD in obedience both in doctrine and conduct. If we are careless in maintaining the doctrines of Scripture or in how we live from day to day we are playing with fire!

Later on in chapter 5 Amos would say, "Seek good and not evil, that you may live; so the LORD God of hosts will be with you, as you have spoken"(14). Seeking after God is at the same time seeking after good and shunning what is evil. It is to seek after justice. Anything else is hypocrisy and insincerity! True religion is doctrine applied. Seeking the guidance of the LORD must be carried forth into deeds of righteousness; deeds that show the love of Christ controls us. Faith without works is dead.

The Israelites did not sincerely love the LORD and therefore they were not able to show true love to their neighbour (1 John 3:10). Where a people seek the LORD you must see a growing love for Him and for each other.

Let us seek the LORD in song, in prayer, in listening and in all we do so that we may be filled with holy enthusiasm for the LORD. "Seek the LORD while He may be found, call upon Him while He is near. Let the wicked forsake his way, and the unrighteous man his thoughts; let him return to the LORD and He will have mercy on him; and to our God, for He will abundantly pardon" (Isaiah 55:6,7). May our whole manner of worship be focussed on God and on all that we have in Christ, to the praise of His glory. The LORD will reward those who seek Him (Hebrews 11:6).

Questions

1. With the help of a good commentary discuss the main point of the sacrifices God prescribed in Leviticus 1-7. How did each of these sacrifices point to the coming Messiah? In which way has Israel failed to see the importance of these offerings?

2. What is the redemptive-historical significance of the places Bethel, Gilgal and Beersheba? How did Israel's misuse of

these places increase their guilt?

3. Why would the prophet encourage the people to offer a sacrifice with leaven? Was this not forbidden by the law (Lev 2:11: 6:17; 7:12-15)?

4. Does Amos 4 & 5 teach us anything about the distinction between the true and false church as confessed in Articles 27-29 of the Belgic Confession? Does this passage legitimize speaking about the church in terms of "pure" and "less pure"?

5. How can we be sure that we are attending the church where the LORD wants us to be? What is wrong with making church membership a matter of personal preference?

6. What is the Biblical background for the various elements of liturgy within your local congregation? Is it wrong to have traditions in worship?

7. Are we permitted to add any elements to our worship services that are not regulated in the Word of the LORD?

8. Compare 1 Kings 12:32,33 with Leviticus 9. What is the difference in the refrain found in these passages?

CHAPTER 7

PREPARE TO MEET YOUR GOD

Reading: Deuteronomy 28:15-35; Amos 4:6-13
Song selection: Psalms 51,57,108,139

Key verse: Amos 4:12
"Therefore thus will I do to you, O Israel;
Because I will do this to you,
Prepare to meet your God, O Israel!"

Throughout the Old and New Testament the LORD reveals Himself to us as longsuffering, patient, slow to anger and abounding in steadfast love. His people constantly stray away from the covenant He established with them and they sin against His commandments. Yet for the sake of His own great Name the LORD restrains His wrath and keeps calling His children to return to Him.

Right to the present the LORD is rich in mercy and patience. If God would deal with us according to our transgressions and sins none of us could stand before the heat of His wrath! The deeper our knowledge of our own sinfulness the more we understand what the apostle Paul writes in Romans 7:18,19, 24, "For I know that in me (that is, in my flesh) nothing good dwells; for to will is present with me, but how to perform what is good I do not find. For the good that I will to do, I do not do; but the evil I will not to do, that I practice. O wretched man that I am! Who will deliver me from this body of death?" Indeed, sin plagues us every day! We all fall short of what the LORD requires of us in His holy Word.

In dealing with sinners we can be so merciless and lacking in patience! We are slow to forgive and quick to condemn. Our God does not treat us in that manner. He knows how prone we are to stumble. Moved with compassion and pity the LORD calls us to find life, communion and blessings with Him.

Nevertheless, the LORD's patience and longsuffering do not exclude His righteousness and justice. He postpones His judgment but He does not cancel it. The LORD warns His people repeatedly that covenant disobedience has dreadful results. Those who ignore the call of the gospel and who harden themselves in sin will one day face God's judgment. This is the message of many of the prophets – including Amos. As a messenger of the LORD, Amos warns the people, both then and now, to break with sin, to hate it and flee from it.

The LORD impresses upon our hearts that we are accountable for our thoughts, our actions and our words. The salvation granted to us in Christ is sufficient to cover all our sins, but this does not mean sin has no consequences. The LORD will judge our actions. Everyone who refuses to heed the call to return to Him will have to give account.

THE CONTEXT OF THIS CALL

Amos 4:12 states, "Therefore thus will I do to you, O Israel, because I will do this to you, prepare to meet your God." When the people of Israel stood at the foot of Mount Sinai to receive the law, they were given three days to get ready to meet the LORD. The Israelites had to consecrate and purify themselves and they had to listen carefully to the instructions given to them, lest they would be consumed by the anger of the LORD. They drew near and stood before the LORD as He declared to them His covenant. They could not come into the presence of this holy and almighty God without following His instructions for a proper preparation.

Similarly, before every Sabbath Day the Israelites were to prepare themselves to come in holy convocation before the LORD. Isaiah encourages the people to prepare themselves for the Sabbath so that this day be used for the LORD and not for their own pleasure. He says, "If you turn away your foot from the Sabbath, from doing your pleasure on My holy day, and call the Sabbath a delight, the holy day of the LORD honorable, and shall honor Him, not doing your own ways, nor finding your own pleasure, nor speaking your own words, then you shall delight yourself in the LORD; and I will cause you to ride on the high hills of the earth, and feed you with the heritage of Jacob your father. The mouth of the LORD has spoken" (Isaiah 58:13,14).

In the New Dispensation the LORD calls us to prepare ourselves to meet Him in worship each Lord's Day and to get ready for the marriage feast of the Lamb on the eternal Sabbath Day. Thus we read the following invocation in Revelation 19, " 'Let us be glad and rejoice and give Him glory, for the marriage of the Lamb has come, and His wife has made herself ready.' And to her it was granted to be arrayed in fine linen, clean and bright, for the fine linen is the righteous acts of the saints."

Scripture also tells us that a believer who has put his house in order, dealing with sin in the way he ought to, can sing, "O God, my heart is steadfast " (Psalm 108:1). The word for steadfast is the same word used in Amos 4:12 for prepared. By the mercy of God, my heart is prepared, it has been made ready, and thus I will sing praises, yes, I will sing praises.

The preparation God calls for in Amos 4:12 is of a different nature than that of Sabbath celebration. The meeting is not for peace but to settle accounts with a disobedient and rebellious people. Just as a mother may say to her misbehaving child, "You had better be prepared to explain your behaviour to your father," so our heavenly Father warns His children that they have some explaining to do! People in the Northern kingdom of Israel will have to explain why they did not return to the LORD but kept going in their own sinful ways and in setting their own norms for worship and social practices.

The call to prepare for a meeting with the LORD is placed within the context of Israel's failure to return to the LORD as stated in verses 6-11. Throughout these verses we hear the same distressing refrain. At the end of verses 6,8,9,10,11 – five times —He repeats the sad news, "'Yet you have not returned to Me', says the LORD." These words reveal to us the purpose the LORD had, and still has, in bringing economic or physical hardship. They are meant to bring us to repentance.

When the LORD gave His people cleanness of teeth and lack of bread, when He smote them with blight and mildew, it wasn't to make life miserable for them but it was an expression of His love. Yet the Northern kingdom of Israel hardened themselves and would not return to the LORD. Politically, socially and economically life in the nation was extremely corrupt. The sin of self-willed worship, as introduced by Jeroboam I, had poisoned everything. They saw no need to return to the LORD because they believed they were doing just fine!

It should not surprise us that returning to the LORD is very difficult. It involves tremendous self-denial. Returning to the LORD is a turning back to the Scriptures and allowing His Word to regulate our thoughts, words, works and worship. Repentance includes pushing away whatever attracts our sinful flesh and letting Christ rule our hearts. Those who repent of their sins must hate them and flee from them, putting to death whatever is earthly in them.

Such reformation and return goes entirely against the grain of our human way of thinking."It means allowing your own kingdom to collapse, letting your old nature die, and attending your own funeral. It means the painful operation of plucking out your eye and cutting off the hand that leads you into sin. It means dying with Christ and being raised with him, in order to follow him in obedience."(Herman Veldkamp, *The Farmer of Tekoa*, p.139). Daily we must come before the LORD with a broken and contrite heart. We must pray fervently with the psalmist, "Create in me a clean heart"(Psalm 51). "Search me, O God, and know my heart; try me, and know my anxieties; and see if there is any wicked way in me, and lead me in the way everlasting" (Psalm 139:23-24).

Confession and repentance are integral components of life in the covenant. What a terrible downward spiral occurs when people let their communion with the living God slip away through disobedience! Amos 4:6-11 describes how Israel made that downward trek. They no longer heard the LORD calling to them. They did not read the warning signs in what He brought upon them.

The LORD gave them cleanness of teeth and lack of bread so that Israel would learn to trust in Him, but they did not return to Him. He chastened them and sought to discipline them by holding back the rain from falling throughout the land. Nevertheless, Israel did not pay attention to what the LORD was teaching them. They kept marching along their own path of self-willed service. The LORD struck their crops with blight, mildew and locusts. That did not shake them either.

The people of the Northern kingdom worshipped the LORD but it was void of any meaning because they did not put what the LORD required of them into practice. When it came right down to it they did not really need Him. They explained all their problems away without taking into account that their economic and political troubles were really of a spiritual nature. The LORD permitted military adversaries to overthrow Israel's cities. Their survival as a nation was truly amazing. They had nothing to boast about even though they were prosperous at the present moment.

During the course of their history the LORD had made some of the people like those of Sodom and Gomorrah. They became a burning waste of salt and sulphur. The Northern kingdom had no reason for boasting because it was like a "firebrand plucked from the burning" (4:11). The LORD, in divine love, snatched them from the fire. He had kept them from total decimation. But even then, Israel had rejected the LORD's gracious provision.

Through the law and via the prophets the LORD laid out in great detail how He would, on the one hand, bless the obedience of His people and, on the other hand, curse their impenitence. For example, consider what we read in Deuteronomy 28. After spelling out the blessings of covenant faithfulness the LORD warns Israel about the consequences of disobedience, "But it shall come to pass, if you do not obey the voice of the LORD your God, to observe carefully all His commandments and His statutes which I command you today, that all these curses will come upon you and overtake you. The LORD will send on you cursing, confusion, and rebuke in all that you set your hand to do, until you are destroyed and until you perish quickly, because of the wickedness of your doings in which you have forsaken me." The list of curses includes disaster and panic (20), pestilence (21), fever and sickness, drought and mildew (22).

It is noteworthy that every punishment described in Amos 4:6-11 corresponds exactly to the curses listed in the law. All that has happened and is about to happen has been solidly explained in the law of the LORD as the just, definite payment and punishment for covenant disobedience.

The LORD always does what He says. Even though we are faithless, He remains faithful to His covenant promises and demands. As we stress the grace of God in Christ we must also emphasize the equally necessary element of required obedience. In addition, we should expect God's judgment upon disobedience to be an integral part of the covenant in the New Dispensation, just as it was in the Old. God's covenant requires it! He cannot let sin or disobedience go unpunished.

THE CONTENT OF THE CALL

If what had happened was not enough, the LORD states in verse 12 that there is yet more to come! "Therefore thus will I do to you, O Israel; because I will do this to you, prepare to meet your God, O Israel."

The word "prepare" anticipates a future event such as a meal. For example, when Joseph saw that Benjamin had come with his brothers to Egypt he told the steward of his house to make preparations for dinner (Genesis 43:16). Preparations are also in order for a military battle. Scripture speaks of the LORD being at war with the ungodly and He calls them to prepare themselves to meet Him. Thus Jeremiah warned the Egyptians of the coming of Nebuchadnezzar king of Babylon. "Stand fast and prepare yourselves, for the sword devours all around you" (Jeremiah 46:14). The LORD used Nebuchadnezzar as His instrument to judge the Egyptians.

In similar fashion, Amos declares to the Northern kingdom that their doom is sure. The LORD is not coming to sit down and dine with His people in a feast of communion but He is about to meet them with a display of His wrath. Since the people of Israel have refused to return to God, they are on the verge of hopelessness. The LORD will unleash all the curses of the covenant upon them. They will feel the full fury of His wrath as His patience and longsuffering come to an end. A people who have strayed will have to appear before the judgment of the LORD of hosts. They stand on their own without the righteousness and salvation of the Messiah.

The situation is grim indeed! The people of the Northern kingdom of Israel are on the edge of the abyss, so to speak. The death toll is about to sound and when it does they will be cut off from all hope.

Note the emphasis, "Prepare to meet *your* God, O Israel." The LORD is not addressing a stranger but again in covenant love reaches out to His children. The LORD reminds them of the relationship He established with them and how He said, "I will be your God and you shall be my people." One last time He sounds the alarm. The LORD calls Israel from the road of eternal death to walk on the way of eternal life. To put it in the words of the prophet Ezekiel, "Therefore I will judge you, O house of Israel, every one according to his ways, says the LORD God. Repent, and turn from all your transgressions, so that iniquity will not be your ruin. Cast away from you all the transgressions which you have committed, and get yourselves a new heart and a new spirit. For why should you die, O house of Israel?" (Ezekiel 18:30,31).

As long as there is no reformation or return to the Word of the LORD, the meeting between the LORD and His people will be very difficult and painful. Israel shows no fruits of faith. They have not adorned their life with godliness. They are not preparing themselves as a bride for her wedding day. Their piety is counterfeit because it has been planted in a garden of self-willed worship.

This is the reason why the LORD calls His people to prepare to meet Him. Israel needs to give account as to why they have fallen so deeply. They must realize they have no one to blame but themselves. God's people will have to answer why they did not keep their side of the covenant by living in obedience. Why did they not respond when God sent to them the prophets and when He forewarned them through plagues and pestilence?

Also today the LORD may meet us with judgment by taking away from us what we have. The LORD took away from the Northern kingdom their status as His chosen people. He sent them into exile and scattered them among the nations. The same happened to Judah at the fall of Jerusalem. Every church which goes its own way will come under God's wrath. On the final day of judgment the LORD will, for the last time, meet those who have spurned His covenant. All who have been placed in the covenant will be confronted by the LORD and all excuses for not returning to His service will be unacceptable. The LORD will not be mocked but will judge all unfaithfulness and disloyalty.

But who then can stand when He appears? For, as we already mentioned, all of us sin and fall short of the glory of God. Can we, who are sinners and inclined to all sorts of evil, prepare ourselves to meet the LORD? Nevertheless, no matter who we are we must be prepared to meet the LORD! For we will all appear before Him either for salvation or condemnation.

As long as the call "prepare to meet your God" is still heard, there is hope. Those who seek their life in Christ, who confess their sins and seek to amend their lives according to God's covenant ordinances do not have to fear the judgment of God. He saved a remnant in Israel and in Judah. The LORD continues to gather to Himself a church chosen to everlasting life. He will vindicate His elect who cry to Him day and night. Through the present work of our Saviour, He is preparing a place where we can meet with Him at an everlasting feast of sweet communion.

Let the candour and earnestness of this passage sink deeply into your soul so that you apply it concretely in your personal life. All false piety, hypocrisy, and self-willed worship will be unmasked. Therefore, be prepared to meet your God! The LORD comes to you every week in the proclamation of the gospel. Coming together as church you are permitted to be in a meeting with the LORD, to hear the gospel of communion in Christ's blood. In the assembly of God's people you already have a foretaste of what is to come. The Lord Jesus is your refuge against the wrath of the LORD since He has accomplished all the obedience required by God's law for you.

May the riches you have received from the LORD never testify against you but draw you closer to Him. Let it be your daily prayer and confession, "Lord come quickly! My heart is steadfast, it is prepared, O my God, since You in Christ have had mercy on me and made my heart ready in the love You prepared ages ago!"

Questions

1. Five times we read in the verses 6-11, "yet you have not returned to me." List the five ways in which the LORD sought to correct Israel's sin.

2. What specific hardships is the LORD speaking about when He says, "I gave you cleanness of teeth...I also withheld rain from you... I blasted you with blight and mildew" (verse 6,7,9)?

3. In the Old Testament drought and economic hardships were covenant curses. How does God withhold His blessings from the church today? Is prosperity to be equated with blessing?

4. Physical and economic hardships were meant to bring the Israelites to their knees before the LORD in true repentance and conversion. Discuss this statement within our contemporary context.

5. Give several examples from Israel's history as to how the LORD plucked His people from the fire (verse 11).

6. What does the Bible teach us regarding our own sinfulness? Is there a need to pray for forgiveness of sins on a daily basis?

7. Sin is never without its consequences. What did the LORD say would be the effects of Israel's sin (Deut 28)?

8. In view of the calling "prepare to meet your God," discuss ways in which we can better prepare ourselves for worship.

9. Can there come a time when we will need to ask the LORD that He bring trouble upon the lives of His people?

CHAPTER 8

THE DAY OF THE LORD WILL BE A DAY OF JUDGMENT

Reading: Amos 5:6-27
Song selection: Psalms 56,75,97

Key verses: Amos 5:18-20
Woe to you who desire the day of the LORD!
For what good is the day of the LORD to you?
It will be darkness, and not light.
It will be as though a man fled from a lion,
And a bear met him!
Or as though he went into the house,
Leaned his hand on the wall,
And a serpent bit him!
Is not the day of the LORD darkness, and not light?
Is it not very dark, with no brightness in it?

$\mathcal{A}$s New Testament church we have become accustomed to pray for the Lord to return. We sing, "Come, Lord Jesus, Maranatha. Thy great day is drawing near." The confessions of the church repeat this in summary. For example in Article 37 of the Belgic Confession we make the following statement of faith, "Therefore we look forward to that great day with a great longing to enjoy to the full the promises of God in Jesus Christ our Lord. Amen. Come, Lord Jesus! (Rev. 22:20)." The same sentiments are echoed in the Heidelberg Catechism. Lord's Day 19 speaks of the comfort we have knowing Christ will come to judge the living and the dead: "In all my sorrow and persecution I lift up my head and eagerly await as judge from heaven the very same person who before has submitted Himself to the judgment of God for my sake."

The more we become aware of our own sinfulness and are confronted with the many hardships of life the more we will long for the day of the LORD and the return of our Lord Jesus Christ. But why then does Amos say, "Woe to you who desire the day of the LORD! For what good is the day of the LORD to you?" The prophecy of Amos seems contradictory. In chapter 4:12 Amos said, "Therefore thus will I do to you, O Israel; because I will do this to you, prepare to meet your God, O Israel!" Now he is telling them not to long for the day of the LORD. Is this logical? Does it make any sense?

It is important to understand Amos is not speaking in generalities. He challenges the religious practices of his day. The people of God in the Northern kingdom of Israel were not living for the LORD –though they thought they were. They considered themselves to be rather pious and God-fearing – bringing their sacrifices, singing the psalms of David, and going through great efforts to display to others that they were deeply religious.

The LORD is not impressed with their religious fervour. He warns those who are quick to express their desire for the LORD's return. Do they have their house in order? Are they truly prepared to meet their God? Amos exhorts those who desire the day of the LORD to realize how God will be coming to meet them.

THE DAY OF THE LORD: A NIGHT WITHOUT DAWN

The message Amos is commissioned to pass on to the people of the Northern kingdom of Israel was not pleasant. The day the people desire will not be a day of salvation and redemption but a day the LORD will punish sin and set things right. It will be a time characterized by darkness, and not light. Amos proclaims, "Is not the day of the LORD darkness, and not light? Is it not very dark, with no brightness in it?"

Light is associated with the LORD, with life and growth. Light spells gospel! When people hear the good news of salvation then the Scriptures declare, "The people who walked in darkness have seen a great light; those who dwelt in the land of the shadow of death, upon them a light has shined" (Isaiah 9:2). In contrast darkness is connected to evil and deeds of wickedness. Those who are estranged from and rebel against the LORD are in darkness. Job 24:13-17 portrays it well, "There are those who rebel against the light; they do not know its ways nor abide in its paths. The murderer rises with the light; he kills the poor and needy; and in the night he is like a thief. The eye of the adulterer waits for the twilight, saying, 'No eye will see me'; and he disguises his face. In the dark they break into houses which they marked for themselves in the daytime; they do not know the light. For the morning is the same to them as the shadow of death; If someone recognizes them, they are in the terrors of the shadow of death."

The Bible describes hell as a place of darkness and gloom. Those who do not use their talents and gifts in the LORD's service will be cast into the outer darkness where people weep and gnash their teeth (Matthew 25:30).

When Amos announces that the day of the LORD is going to be a day of darkness he does not necessarily mean that the sun will be blotted out and the moon and the stars will not shine anymore, but that the blessing of the LORD will be withdrawn and men and women will be without the Light of life. When people are in the dark they are without the LORD. God's countenance does not shine upon them and they do not have peace. The day of the LORD will be a day in which those who do not believe in Jesus Christ will be cut off from Him eternally.

REASONS WHY THE LORD IS DISPLEASED

One of the reasons for God's displeasure is corruption in worship. Amos interrupts Israel's busyness and the activity at Israel's centres of worship to announce the LORD's reaction to all that is going on.

The LORD is very negative about what His people are doing. They think they are extremely pious and are doing Him great favours but the LORD responds, "I hate, I despise your feasts, I take no delight in your solemn assemblies, I will not accept your burnt offerings and cereal offerings. I will not look upon your peace offerings. Take away from me the noise of your songs" (paraphrase 5:21-23).

Taken together, these statements make clear that the LORD's rejection of Israel's worship is total. He does not like the sight, the smell or the sound of what is going on in the religious sanctuaries because the piety of His people is not real but self-designed.

Worship in the Northern kingdom of Israel was not acceptable. It reinforced the people's own pride and inflated their own reputations. They were filled with themselves and thus the soul had gone out of worship. Rather than exalting the holy name of the LORD they clamoured to put themselves in the foreground.

The second reason why the day of the LORD would not be a day of light but of darkness had to do with the manner in which the people conducted themselves in their daily life, in their business transactions and dealings with others. The small farmer was being charged an excessive amount for the rental of land and the rich owners were taking more than their fair share of the crop. They took advantage of the poor to enrich their own coffers. When the poor went to court to complain their words were ignored, even though they were true. Furthermore, those making judgments were accepting bribes, favouring the wealthy and powerful.

The citizens of the Northern kingdom of Israel no longer lived in complete harmony with God's commandments and ordinances. Yet they still thought that the LORD was with them. They believed that they could say, "The LORD is with us" (5:14) and they looked forward to the time He would be with them in a spectacular way, articulated by the words "the day of the LORD" (5:18). Israel trusted all was well between them and the LORD. Without any qualms they could walk together in covenant communion and desire the day of the LORD.

Such thinking was based on the fact that Israel was thriving politically, socially and economically. Thus the contemporaries of Amos did what so many to the present have done – confusing success with blessing. All their prosperity made them think they were being blessed by the LORD. The future could only get better and become more glorious. They were convinced in their own minds that when the "day of the LORD" arrived the success they now enjoyed would be multiplied and perfected. Everything negative and everyone who opposed them would be destroyed. Why not look forward to the day of the LORD? God would certainly reward them for their deeds. They believed the day of the LORD would bring Israel much good. Surely the heathen peoples should be afraid of the day of the LORD, but not the enlightened Israelites!

As the Northern kingdom falls further and deeper into the pit of sin, wisdom becomes increasingly scarce. The people of God no longer have the sense to see where their sins are leading them. They have become blind to the fact that their prosperity is killing them. Though they prospered economically they have become spiritually impoverished. "For they are a nation void of counsel, nor is there any understanding in them. Oh, that they were wise, that they understood this, that they would consider their latter end!"(Deut 32:28,29).

Amos cannot share their optimism. He cannot keep silent but he must speak out against their faulty reasoning. The people have a very shallow perception of the LORD, of His holiness, greatness and majesty. In three consecutive verses (14,15,16) Amos draws Israel's attention to the God before whom they stand. The God of the covenant is not their "buddy" but He is LORD God of hosts. Israel can only say with certainty that the LORD is with them if they hate evil and love good and establish justice in the gate (5:15).

The prophet of the LORD attempts to shake the people of the Northern kingdom out of their complacency. Glorying in the benefits of the covenant while forgetting the demands of the relationship is an abomination in the eyes of the LORD, "Woe to you who desire the day of the LORD! For what good is the day of the LORD to you? It will be darkness, and not light" (vs. 18).

As people of God we are called to evaluate our religious activities in the light of the Word of God. For what the LORD desires above everything is for justice and righteousness to roll through the land like a surging stream (5:24). Pursuing justice, as a Biblical concept, is more than being fair. It is to look after and defend the poor, the widowed, the fatherless, and those who are alone in the communion of saints (Isaiah 10:1-4). Justice is looking after the needs of the elderly and those who are new to the community of believers (Deut. 24:19-22; Lev. 19:32). This is what true religion is about. If justice existed and had been administered within the gates, the poor would have been looked after properly and the covenant people would have enjoyed the blessings of the LORD.

Although the people of the Northern kingdom were extremely busy with all sorts of religious activities they were missing the very essence of it. They invested their time and energy in building fancy homes for themselves, in establishing successful businesses. They felt they had a right to treat themselves to a little luxury. The people worked hard at planting and caring for their vineyards and crops but they neglected the essential ingredients of covenant living: "to do justly, to love mercy, and to walk humbly with your God" (Micah 6:8).

Once again the people in the Northern kingdom of Israel are admonished to repent of their sins. Their whole attitude and the way they think must change. If Israel had been standing in the right relationship with the LORD, had kept His covenant ordinances, had been faithful in their pursuit of righteousness, holiness and justice, the day of the LORD would be a day of light and not darkness. Since they were not doing this, the day they longed for would actually be a day of doom and gloom.

Amos was not the first prophet and would not be the last to speak of the day of the LORD. For those who cleave to the LORD in faith, hope and love there is nothing to fear when the LORD appears on His great day. Yet fear should fill the hearts of those who do not live in a right relationship with the LORD. In the same vein Zephaniah writes in chapter 1:14-17, "The great day of the LORD is near, it is near and hastens quickly. The noise of the day of the LORD is bitter, there the mighty men shall cry out. That day is a day of wrath, a day of trouble and distress, a day of devastation and desolation, a day of darkness and gloominess, a day of clouds and thick darkness, a day of trumpet and alarm against the fortified cities and against the high towers. I will bring distress upon men, and they shall walk like blind men, because they have sinned against the LORD..."

There is only one bright spot for Israel in the portrait of the coming darkness: the day of the LORD has not yet come. The LORD in great compassion calls the Northern kingdom to return to the ways of the covenant. Thus in the midst of this bleak picture, Amos does not hesitate to appeal for the people's good response: "Take away from Me the noise of your songs, for I will not hear the melody of your stringed instruments. But let justice run down like water, and righteousness like a mighty stream" (5:23, 24).

What Amos communicates is not merely a word spoken in a by-gone era which has nothing to do with us today. In fact, the Word of the LORD speaks more powerfully than it ever did before. For we know Jesus Christ who came into the world as the Light, the Truth and the Life. Our Lord Jesus Christ said, "For what profit is it to a man if he gains the whole world, and is himself destroyed or lost?" (Luke 9:25). What does it profit us to be successful in business, to be good at our job, to have a Christian school, to send our children to catechism, to get involved in sports and entertainment, etc., if we do not strive for the holiness without which no one can see the LORD, if we do not let justice and righteousness flow like a surging stream? Performing religious duties to gain a name for ourselves or out of custom or tradition will bring us into judgment. No one will be able to escape the punishment of the LORD. If we do not use what the LORD has given us it will only testify against us.

THE DAY OF THE LORD: A DANGER WITHOUT ESCAPE

The Bible speaks of the day of the LORD because the time of judgment is fixed and therefore is as unescapable as any other day of history. The day of the LORD is coming. No one can run away from it.

Amos gives a vivid picture depicting how the darkness of the day of the LORD is unavoidable. With a few short phrases the prophet paints a highly charged and emotional scene. A man taking a walk through the forest is suddenly faced by the king of the animal world: a fierce lion. Filled with fear he turns and runs as fast as he can. His heart beats wildly. Sweat pours down from his face. After running some distance he looks behind him and sees that he has managed to escape the fangs of the lion. Sighing with relief, he does not realize a bear has heard him and now stands in front of him, ready to attack. Again he faces death, and again he must muster up all his strength and flee for his life. He hears the animal panting behind him. Trembling with fear he makes a mad dash for home. Completely exhausted, he stumbles inside and bolts the door. He is safe at last. Out of breath, he leans against the wall to support his body that has been sapped of all its strength. But just where he puts his hand, there is a crack in the wall. Concealed in the wall is a small poisonous snake. The snake bites his hand! The man cries out in surprise and fright. Horror fills his face as he sees his hand begin to swell. The poison works its way through his body quickly. His colour changes to ashen gray. He dies a horrible death all by himself in his own home (Veldkamp p.174).

This is an awful story, isn't it? The man escaped a lion and a bear but a small snake kills him in a place where he had gone to find refuge. He had not expected the danger to be in his own home. Via this powerful portrait the LORD warns His people not to think they are secure in Zion, in the church of the living God. They will not escape the wrath of the LORD or the darkness of the day of the LORD by leaning on their status as church. The people may feel secure in Zion but the LORD will reach them even in the city where He chose to put His name.

The day of the LORD is coming! He who thinks he can escape danger is deceiving himself. The imagery of the lion, bear and snake underline the first three words of the text, "Woe to you!" Amos' contemporaries were optimistic and believed everything would be all right. There were no dangers on the horizon. They were God's people and therefore they did not worry in the least about the future. But it is clear that being a member of the church and of the covenant is no license to sin. Complacency only feeds false hope. When the day of the LORD comes He will turn and be the enemy of all who despised His Word and who did not keep His commandments.

The only escape from danger is in the LORD. Those who seek the

Lord and find their salvation in Jesus Christ will not be ashamed. Holiness is not a cloak or a mask we put on for special occasions but a lifestyle that involves our actions and emotions. "Seek good and not evil, that you may live; so the Lord God of hosts will be with you, as you have spoken. Hate evil, love good..." (5:14,15).

This chapter speaks much of darkness. Yet in the darkness the light of God's grace shines through. We today know our Lord Jesus Christ experienced the darkness of God's punishment for us when He was forsaken by His Father. The Lord laid on Him our iniquities and our unrighteousness. Those who are in Christ have the Light and do not have to fear the darkness of the day of the Lord.

Once we were darkness, now we are light in the Lord. Therefore we must walk in the light (Ephesians 5:8). Our text is a warning to all of us. Do not be complacent or careless or satisfied with your own religiosity. "Seek good and not evil, that you may live; so the Lord God of hosts will be with you, as you have spoken. Hate evil, love good; establish justice in the gate..." (vs 14,15). Flee to the crucified Christ. Being hid in Him is the only *safe* way you can meet God and the only way you can desire and long for the day of the Lord. It is the only way you can pray without fear in your heart, "Come Lord Jesus, Maranatha!"

Questions

1. How can we look forward to the day of the Lord in the confidence it will be a day of blessing and rejoicing?

2. In which way does Psalm 73 indicate that blessing and success are not to be equated with one another?

3. What does the phrase, "He turns the shadow of death into morning" mean (5:8)?

4. What is the significance of the reference to the star constellations Pleiades and Orion (5:8)?

5. How must true religion manifest its reality in our life? By contrast with verse 10-13, the mark of a changed person is his willingness to listen to the voice of God's law. Discuss.

6. Verse 10 says, "They hate the one who rebukes in the gate." Why does this happen so often in the course of history?

7. What does the LORD require of His people to have the assurance that He will be with them (5:14)?

8. What is meant by "the day of the LORD" (5:18,20)? What did the people believe would occur on that day, and how was this different from what Amos foretold would happen?

9. The LORD uses a powerful metaphor in verse 19 involving a lion, bear and snake. What is the point that is being driven home?

10. Why can there be no light for the Northern kingdom of Israel on the day of the LORD? How are the words of chapter 5:18-20 a strong warning to the church of the 21st century?

11. Look at the picture of worship in 5:22-23. What's wrong with this picture? What do these verses teach us regarding our practices and traditions in worship?

12. Verse 24 says, "But let justice run down like water, and righteousness like a mighty stream." How can we be sure this is happening within our local congregations?

13. What message is the LORD conveying in 5:25 by bringing up the lack of sacrifices and offerings during the forty years of wandering in the wilderness?

14. Who were Sikkuth (Sakkuth) and Chiun (Kaiwan)? Why are they mentioned in 5:26?

CHAPTER 9

AMOS LAMENTS THE RELIGIOUS COMPLACENCY OF GOD'S CHOSEN PEOPLE

Reading: Amos 5:1-3; 6:1-14
Song Selection: Psalms 4,6,34,49

Key Verses: Amos 6:1-10
Woe to you who are at ease in Zion,
And trust in Mount Samaria,
Notable persons in the chief nation,
To whom the house of Israel comes!
Go over to Calneh and see;
And from there go to Hamath the great;
Then go down to Gath of the Philistines.
Are you better than these kingdoms?
Or is their territory greater than your territory?

Woe to you who put far off the day of doom,
Who cause the seat of violence to come near;
Who lie on beds of ivory,
Stretch out on your couches,

Eat lambs from the flock
And calves from the midst of the stall;
Who sing idly to the sound of stringed instruments,
And invent for yourselves musical instruments like David;
Who drink wine from bowls,
And anoint yourselves with the best ointments,
But are not grieved for the affliction of Joseph.
Therefore they shall now go captive as the first of the
captives,
And those who recline at banquets shall be removed.
The LORD *GOD has sworn by Himself,*
The LORD *God of hosts says:*
"I abhor the pride of Jacob,
And hate his palaces;
Therefore I will deliver up the city
And all that is in it."

Then it shall come to pass, that if ten men remain in one
house, they shall die. And when a relative of the dead,
with one who will burn the bodies, picks up the bodies to
take them out of the house, he will say to one inside the
house, "Are there any more with you?" Then someone
will say, "None." And he will say, "Hold your tongue!
For we dare not mention the name of the LORD*."*

When Amos was commissioned by the LORD to prophesy in the Northern kingdom of Israel, he wasn't given a very happy message to deliver: the Israelites continue to live in sin and thus write up their own death notice; they are attending their own funeral.

All throughout this prophecy statements are made expressing the grief and lamentation of one who is at a funeral. Amos writes in chapter 1:2, "The LORD roars from Zion, and utters His voice from Jerusalem; the pastures of the shepherds mourn, and the top of Carmel withers." In chapter 5:1-3 he says, "Hear this word which I take up against you, a lamentation, O house of Israel: The virgin of

Israel has fallen; she will rise no more. She lies forsaken on her land; there is no one to raise her up. For thus says the LORD God: 'The city that goes out by a thousand shall have a hundred left, and that which goes out by a hundred shall have ten left to the house of Israel.'" Israel is personified as a young virgin who has died. Amos calls his audience to join in lamenting her death. A final reference to mourning and lamentation is found in chapter 9:5, "The LORD God of hosts, He who touches the earth and it melts, and all who dwell there mourn..." (See also chapter 8:7-10).

In the ancient world, professional mourners were hired to attend funerals. Central to their sounds was the cry "woe" or "alas." This, too, is found in the prophecy of Amos, and particularly in chapter 5:18 and 6:1, "Woe to you who desire the day of the LORD! For what good is the day of the LORD to you! ...Woe to you who are at ease in Zion, and trust in Mount Samaria." Just as it used to be a custom to have the bells of a church toll when someone died so the "woeful" sound of the weepers would elicit the question, "Who has died?"

When Amos pronounced a "woe," the effect on those who heard it would have been chilling. It was like reading your own name in the obituary column of the local newspaper! Yes, woe to those "for whom the bell tolls" (Ernest Hemingway). Through Amos the LORD announced the death of a people who had fallen asleep and laid themselves to rest in a grave of religious complacency.

WHAT COMPLACENCY HAS DONE TO GOD'S PEOPLE

"Woe to you who are at ease in Zion, and trust in Mount Samaria" is the mournful cry of the farmer of Tekoa. Amos encourages the people to weep with him for those who are at ease and feel secure because in reality they are dead in their sins.

Being at ease, and feeling secure, is not necessarily a negative or bad thing. Rest and ease are things to be desired in the Christian life. There are verses in Scripture that promise rest and invite us to relax and enjoy what the LORD has given to us. Our Lord Jesus Christ said, "Come to me, all you who labour and are heavy laden, and I will give you rest" (Matthew 11:28). Christ summons us to lay down our heavy burdens at His feet and enjoy the rest He gives, to feel safe and secure with Him. Through the prophet Jeremiah, the LORD comforts His people with these words, "But do not fear, O my servant Jacob, and do not be dismayed, O Israel! For behold, I will save you from afar, and your offspring from the land of their captivity; Jacob shall return, have rest and be at ease; no one shall make him afraid" (Jeremiah 46:27). As believers, we are promised a Sabbath rest, a time when we can enter into the rest of the LORD. Christians are promised rest and peace in Christ. Isaiah 32:17 says, "The work of righteousness will be peace, and the effect of righteousness, quietness and assurance forever."

What brings death to a people is false security. There is no rest for the wicked (Isaiah 57:20,21), for those who live in a way that is not pleasing to the LORD. Those who are falsely at ease are like a person who lays himself down to rest in his own coffin.

Even though this prophecy is directed to the Northern kingdom of Israel, Amos targets specifically those who trust in Zion and who feel secure in Samaria. Zion was, at that time, the legitimate continuation of the covenant people of the LORD. However, the inhabitants of Zion should not think themselves excluded from punishment when they follow the same sinful patterns of the Northern kingdom of Israel.

The people of Judah, and the religious leaders in particular, felt at ease and rather smug because they knew Zion had been chosen by the LORD to be His dwelling place. They counted on the LORD's grace and blessings. Zion had a rich heritage, being the place where the temple was located, where the priests offered sacrifices and where the throne of David was found. Had not the LORD promised redemption would come to Zion? Had He not said the Messiah would come forth from the royal line of David? Instead of being thankful for God's grace, Judah became complacent. They thought judgment would come to others but not to them.

Amos warns the "notable persons in the chief of the nation, to whom the house of Israel comes" (6:1). Notable persons are those in leadership positions who are "mentioned by name" (Numbers 1:17). These are the leaders to whom the people of Israel come for the resolving of disputes and for counsel in the perplexities of life (Exodus 18:16). The "notable persons" in the covenant nation have not put the well-being of the people of God as their priority. They have made self-pampering their number one goal and consequently have become blind to the fact that they are leading the nation down a road to destruction and ruin (6:3-6).

Amos tackles the same smugness and false sense of security that Jeremiah opposes in his prophecy. As the LORD's servant, Jeremiah was commissioned to say, "Stand in the gate of the LORD's house, and proclaim there this word, and say, 'Hear the word of the LORD, all you of Judah who enter in at these gates to worship the LORD!' Thus says the LORD of hosts, the God of Israel: 'Amend your ways and your doings, and I will cause you to dwell in this place. Do not trust in these lying words, saying, 'The temple of the LORD, the temple of the LORD, the temple of the LORD are these'" (Jeremiah 7:1-4).

The prophet from Tekoa takes aim at those who are at ease in Zion but he also directs his comments to the capital of the Northern kingdom, the city of Samaria – at those who feel secure for different reasons. The city of Samaria became established as a centre of wealth and power. The inhabitants of Samaria relied on their own strength and trusted in their military power. This is why the prophet speaks of Mount Samaria. The city of Samaria was strategically located on top of a hill with steep sides. It was protected by thick walls that could hardly be approached by battering rams because of its elevation. Thus Samaria became a symbol of Israel's false security.

Whereas the people of Judah trusted in the fact that they had the temple of the LORD, the people of the Northern kingdom leaned on their military strength. Both trusted in their own sufficiency. The LORD challenges those who trust in Zion and in Samaria to look at the cities of Calneh, Hamath, and Gath – cities that were at one time strong fortifications and centres of worship for the heathen nations. No one was present to save these cities when the LORD came to punish them. Judah and Israel will end up the same as these cities if they do not repent of their pride and arrogance. There is no security in military strength. Nor is there reason to be a proud member of the church because whatever we have has been given to us by grace through Jesus Christ.

Amos encourages his audience to take up a lament! The pride of Jacob, the false security of Samaria and the ease of Zion are killing and destroying what the LORD has established. Samaria's ruin and exile are already certain. Nevertheless, it may be that the LORD will be gracious to a remnant (5:15).

The cry of mourning is not only taken up for those who have become at ease, but also for those who delay taking action on what the LORD requires, who keep telling themselves, "We will change our ways tomorrow. Then we will give up our sinful ways." The prophet warns, "Woe to you who put far off the day of doom, who cause the seat of violence to come near." A lamentation is sounded against the religious complacency of those who are self-indulgent, "Who lie on beds of ivory, stretch out on your couches, eat lambs from the flock, and calves from the midst of the stall..."(vs. 4).

Becoming comfortable with our own self-designed lifestyle, delaying what we are supposed to do and indulging in the pursuit or enjoyment of material goods is to "lie on beds of ivory, stretching out on couches..." The lives of such people centre on themselves and their recreation. After all, why should God mind? They present to Him their offerings and go through all the motions of religious activity. Amos warns that such behaviour is the death of spiritual life.

Within the Christian church there are always those who trust in outward symbols of religion, such as church membership, baptism and public profession of faith. Nevertheless, church attendance, public profession of faith, participation at the Lord's Supper or involvement in church activities do not make you any more a Christian than working in your garden makes you a flower. What we have been given must be accepted in faith. Religion is a relationship with the LORD and with His people made possible through the saving work of Christ. Rituals and performance may never become a substitute for holiness and knowledge of the LORD. Religion is emptied of its power if there is no living communion and true fellowship with God.

All our help and trust is to be in the LORD. When the people of God place their trust in God the results are powerful and positive. Listen, for example, to what we read in 1 Chronicles 5:20, "...they cried out to God in the battle. He heeded their prayer, because they put their trust in Him."

Living in an environment similar to that experienced by the

Northern kingdom of Israel – a time of wealth and prosperity – we may be feeling so comfortable and relaxed about the way things are going that we coast through life and put off genuine change. We have heard it all and have stored up the doctrines of Scripture in our minds and thus we think we can afford to take it easy. Being partakers of the grace the LORD promises to His people we may have the tendency to be satisfied with the status quo. Seldom do we cry out for the mercy of God in Christ because we have become desensitized to sin. How often do we experience any sense of being broken, of coming before the LORD with a contrite heart and spirit? Peace is only truly ours when we are bonded in a relationship of love with the Triune God.

Are you at ease in Zion? Mourn and weep because of your sins, lest you are called to mourn for your own spiritual death. Do not put off dealing with spiritual matters until later. Do not fool yourself. If you do not do it now, do you really think you will do it later? Waiting until later may be too late. Pray that the LORD will give you a holy uneasiness so that you will mourn and grieve over the presence of sin in your personal life and in the church. Seek the LORD who redeemed you with His own blood.

WHERE COMPLACENCY LEAVES GOD'S PEOPLE

The people to whom Amos prophesied were arrogant, proud, self-indulgent, careless and indifferent. They thought they had a right to treat themselves with the money they had earned. As they accumulated riches their generosity decreased. The life of this people had become totally empty and their religion was void of any meaning. The people God had called to covenant communion were drifting into hell, humming worthless songs.

Amos attacks both luxury and drunkenness at the same time. Those who drink wine from bowls (basins) similar to those used before the altar in the tabernacle (Num 7:13). These bowls were very large and were probably made of costly metal and design.

God's covenant people had knowledge of the best wines and it flowed excessively and liberally at their social events. Israel bathed in the luxury of fine clothing and oil because the emphasis was all on outward appearance, but the inward beauty of a heart set on fire for the true service of the LORD was missing. They enjoyed great worship, and they delighted in artistic originality. Israel was content to go through the motions of religious duty while really caring only for themselves.

The LORD says, "This is not a time for rejoicing and celebration. Where is your grief? The house of Joseph is dead." The Northern kingdom of Israel is about to go into exile and be dispersed among the nations, never again to be known as the special people of the LORD. This people is proud and therefore anyone knowing the ways of the LORD could have asked of them, "Why are you not in sackcloth and ashes? Why are you not mourning the death of a relationship?" But Israel's heart was unmoved by the terrible state of the church. They were too busy with themselves to care.

The pride and arrogance of Jacob is abhorrent. They have no humility. Israel should know what to expect. The "therefore" of verse 7 should not come as a surprise, "Therefore they shall now go captive as the first of the captives..." Those who prided themselves in being leaders will lead the people in a (funeral) procession into exile.

This chapter has one solemn message: the judgment of the LORD is inevitable. The people of God are bringing destruction upon themselves because of sin. Chapter 5:27 announced the punishment of exile, " 'Therefore I will send you into captivity beyond Damascus,' says the LORD, whose name is the God of hosts." That threat is repeated in chapter 6:7 and amplified in 6:14, " 'But, behold, I will raise up a nation against you, O house of Israel,' says the LORD God of hosts; 'and they will afflict you from the entrance of Hamath to the valley of the Arabah.' "

The prosperity of the Northern kingdom had gone to their heads. Such sinful human pride displeases the LORD and kindles His wrath. The omnipotent, sovereign covenant God is roused to anger and will not leave it unpunished. All those who exalt themselves will be humbled (Luke 14:11).

Selfish and sinful human pride manifests its ugly head throughout history in various forms. Therefore we must take careful note of what the LORD says in verse 8, "The LORD has sworn by Himself, the LORD God of hosts says: 'I abhor the pride of Jacob, and hate his palaces; therefore I will deliver up the city and all that is in it.' "

The LORD presents a bleak and horrifying illustration of what happens to those who remain at ease after His wrath descends upon them. Their prosperity will be brought to ruin when the LORD comes to judge them. Amos gives a description of the city of Samaria after the LORD has passed through it with His fearful judgments. If some people have hidden in a house hoping to escape the invading armies, they will not succeed.

Amos tells of a house occupied by ten men huddled together in terror because of the siege conditions. Those who once were well-padded are now skin over bones. The prophet also sees a relative entering into a house with an assistant to burn the bodies of those who have passed away. The word translated "relative," basically means "loved one," and could have been a relative or even a close friend. The very presence of a "burner" already makes the picture repulsive. Cremation was considered an abomination in Israel.

As the relative and his assistant enter the home, they find many dead stretched out on their ivory couches with vacant eyes wide open. If this were not eerie enough, suddenly the relative and the "undertaker" hear from the innermost parts of the house the voice of a survivor! The relative whispers, "Who's that? Is there anyone else who is still alive?" The man replies that he is the lone survivor. As soon as the kinsmen hears the answer he says, "Hush! Be quiet!" and then proceeds to warn the survivor not to call upon the name of the LORD. The relative appeals for silence because he is superstitious. If the survivor would elaborate on his plight, he might mention the name of the LORD and thus cause God's curses to come down on the three men who are presently in the house.

Ironically, this calamity has come upon them because they have refused to acknowledge the Name of the LORD. Desperate as the situation is, the relative will not turn to the LORD for help.

Note further the irony! Those who prided themselves in being number one among the nations (6:1), will be the first to go into captivity (6:7). Pride has filled their hearts and pride will be their ruin. Those who once stretched themselves upon their couches and ivory beds now lie there as corpses unable to enjoy any of their luxury. Those who anointed themselves with the finest oils, with the best ointments they could find, pollute the rooms with the stench of death. The kinsman is so afraid of what the LORD might do if he discovers them, he would rather not have the name of the LORD mentioned at all. He is gripped by fear. Again how ironic and how awful!

At one time the people were very free in using the name of the LORD without really thinking about what they were saying or doing. Very carelessly they worshipped the LORD and called upon His name. They spoke of Him as if He were their best friend. At present they do not turn to the LORD or call upon Him for help in confession of their own guilt.

The kinsman of the dead family is filled with the wrong kind of fear. He does not stand in awe of or revere the living God because he loves Him. The relative of the deceased is afraid he, too, might be killed. Furthermore, his fear of God comes too late! Had he feared and honoured the LORD by listening to the message proclaimed by Amos he could have found his comfort and consolation with the LORD in this time of grief.

When the LORD is your strength and your salvation you will want to call upon His name in the day of trouble. Why be afraid to call upon Him who is your only hope? We use the name of the LORD every day. We call upon Him in our prayers, we speak of Him in worship, we read of His ways in Scripture. Let that familiarity not breed contempt. The name of the LORD has been revealed for our salvation! This is what life is all about!

The name of the LORD spells salvation, forgiveness of sins, the renewal of our heart, the glory of our life. That holds true all the more for us who have come to know the name of our Saviour, Jesus Christ. Blessed are the people who confess the glory of this name and do not silence anyone from speaking about Him in life or death because in the name of the LORD we find refuge at all times. "The name of the LORD is a strong tower, the righteous flee into it and are safe" (Proverbs 18:10).

Questions

1. What is a proper way of being at ease and feeling secure? Give scriptural examples to back up your answer.

2. In which way did Judah and Israel show that they were at ease with a false sense of security?

3. Those who trust in themselves or place their confidence in worldly security trust in vain. Why are we so susceptible to seeking our trust in ourselves and other creatures rather than in the LORD alone?

4. The people of the Northern kingdom of Israel seemed to be oblivious to Amos' warning of destruction. Why are they so self-assured? What needed to happen to break people out of their false sense of security?

5. Why was it necessary that a lament be taken up for God's people? In which way could this have been a positive experience (think of the nature of true repentance)?

6. There is a time in which we must grieve and lament the plight of the church. What, for example, do some of the Psalms and the book of Lamentations teach us about this?

7. What is the significance of the question in verse 2, "Are you better than these kingdoms?"

8. What were the consequences of putting off the day of doom (verse 3)?

9. How were the songs that were sung at Israel's feasts different from those composed by David? What does this tell us about our own choices of music (verse 5)?

10. Does Amos condemn luxury and affluence or does he have

something else on his mind when he says, "Woe to you who put far off the day of doom, who cause the seat of violence to come near; who lie on beds of ivory, stretch out on your couches, eat lambs from the flock and calves from the midst of the stall?"

11. Why is it always a danger for God's people to substitute religious symbols and rituals for real holiness and knowledge of God?

12. How can we grow stronger in the LORD and avoid the idolatry of putting other things, persons and priorities on par with our relationship with the LORD?

13. What is the significance of the "story" in verses 9 & 10?

14. Why was it so wrong that the relative of the deceased did not dare mention the name of the LORD (verse 10)? How should we make proper use of His name? How should the proper usage of God's name affect the manner in which the children of the church are educated?

15. What are the metaphors in 6:12 trying to convey regarding the reason for the coming destruction?

16. Explain the significance of 2 Timothy 3:1-9 in the context of what the LORD has made known to us in Amos 6.

CHAPTER 10

THE CONFLICT BETWEEN TRUE AND FALSE LEADERSHIP IN ISRAEL

Reading: Deuteronomy 23:9-22; Amos 7:1-9
Song Selection: Psalms 50,97,144

Key verses: Amos 7:10-17
*Then Amaziah the priest of Bethel sent to Jeroboam king
of Israel, saying, "Amos has conspired against you in the
midst of the house of Israel. The land is not able to bear
all his words. For thus Amos has said:
'Jeroboam shall die by the sword,
And Israel shall surely be led away captive
From their own land.'"
Then Amaziah said to Amos:*

*"Go, you seer!
Flee to the land of Judah.
There eat bread,
And there prophesy.
But never again prophesy at Bethel,*

For it is the king's sanctuary,
And it is the royal residence."

Then Amos answered, and said to Amaziah:
"I was no prophet,
Nor was I a son of a prophet,
But I was a sheepbreeder
And a tender of sycamore fruit.
Then the LORD *took me as I followed the flock,*
And the LORD *said to me,*
Go, prophesy to My people Israel.'
Now therefore, hear the word of the LORD*:*
You say, 'Do not prophesy against Israel,
And do not spout against the house of Isaac.'

"Therefore thus says the LORD*:*
Your wife shall be a harlot in the city;
Your sons and daughters shall fall by the sword;
Your land shall be divided by survey line;
You shall die in a defiled land;
And Israel shall surely be led away captive
From his own land.'"

*T*his passage tells of a confrontation between a prophet and a priest. Amos, a prophet from Judah, was not a man equipped with any training in rhetoric or public speaking. He is confronted by Amaziah, a prestigious priest at Bethel, who tells him to mind his own business. Amaziah is chief of staff and minister of religious affairs, having the top job in the place where the royal family worships. He is an upper class official in the Northern kingdom of Israel.

When Jeroboam the son of Nebat led the revolt that caused the split between the Northern kingdom of Israel and the Southern kingdom of Judah, he established Bethel as one of the centres of worship. He wanted to keep the people away from Jerusalem and from the religious feast days that were celebrated there. He also created his own rules, determining who would serve as priests. Several years later, during the reign of Jeroboam II, Amaziah is the appointed priest of Bethel.

Amos meets Amaziah in Bethel with a message from the LORD concerning Israel's future. The message causes a clash, not of two personalities, but of truth versus error. This is a confrontation between the Word of the LORD and self-willed religion. What is revealed to us may not be brushed over lightly. We are directed to the basics of covenant living. The Word of the LORD must permeate every aspect and area of life and may not be silenced. For the voice of true prophecy directs us to Christ and His redeeming work. If what is heard is rejected or falls on deaf ears, it will not go well with us. We may plant our crops, work long hours, and go through the motions of worship, but the blessing of the LORD will not rest upon us.

THE COMPLAINT TO THE KING

Throughout the first 6 chapters of this book, the prophet Amos boldly proclaimed the message that the LORD will come to judge the disobedience of the Northern kingdom of Israel. In chapter 7 he explains why he is so sure that what he was commissioned to say will happen. Israel's downfall is certain because they do not listen to the Word of the LORD. The people of God are very busy performing all sorts of religious rituals and therefore they are not worried in the least about the day of the LORD. Yet the LORD warns them that they will be punished and will go into exile because they have constructed their own pattern of worship. The people of God may be religious, but they are not obedient.

Amos spoke boldly of Israel's certain doom. This is what the LORD had shown him in five separate visions. These visions demonstrated a clear movement from bad to worse. In the first two visions, the swarm of locusts and the fire, the LORD relents and declares it will not happen. But in the next three visions, the plumb line (7:7-9), the basket of summer fruit (8:1-3) and the destruction of the altar (9:1-4), the judgment of the LORD is unalterable and final. Amos no longer appeals for mercy.

These visions had originally been given to Amos so that he

might know his task. Now they are passed on to the people so that they might know Amos was not proclaiming his own ideas but was speaking according to what the LORD had shown him. These visions also serve as a last appeal to the people to repent from their sins.

In the first vision Amos sees a cloud of locusts destroying the work of a whole growing season. The plague is of deadly proportions placing the entire population in danger of starvation. The hand of the LORD causes this plague to come upon the people. It is a judgment consistent with what the LORD revealed to Moses (Deut 28:42). Israel had it in writing!

As a farmer, Amos understood how devastating a locust plague could be. In a few short hours these creatures can turn a thriving crop into a disaster area. Just as the locusts destroy the crops many had laboured over, so the LORD will destroy Israel, even though they had spent many hours performing religious rituals.

What is Amos' response? He turns to the LORD and prays for forgiveness because the number of God's chosen is already small. The word "small" is used in the Old Testament to underscore Israel's election by God's sovereign grace (Gen 32:9-12; Deut 7:6-8). The people of Israel have no rights or credentials to parade their own superiority. Amos appeals upon God's covenant mercy to restore helpless Israel. The prophet who was called to proclaim the LORD's judgment utters a priestly prayer entreating God to remember His mercy. He is a true man of God in that he has compassion for a people that are heading for perdition.

Earlier in Israel's history, Moses had interceded with the LORD and on the basis of God's covenant mercy had asked for forgiveness. Now, in a later time, Amos makes the same prayer. Rather than appealing to the LORD's greatness, he bases his prayer on the fact that Jacob is so small. Israel may think quite highly of themselves but this plague puts matters into perspective. They are not as "big" as they think. In response to Amos' prayer, the LORD calls off His judgment with the announcement, "It shall not be."

The second vision is worse than the first. A terrible fire ravishes the land and the great deep. The image is that of an invading army which burns up land and sea as it goes. The devastation described echoes what is written in Deut 32:22, "For a fire is kindled in My anger, and shall burn to the lowest hell; it shall consume the earth with her increase, and set on fire the foundations of the mountains." It also reminds us of the repeated threat of God's judgment as predicted in chapter 1. At the beginning of this prophecy the LORD had said He would send a fire into the house of Hazael and the walls of Gaza and Tyre (1:4,7,10).

Again the meaning is obvious and the prophet implores the LORD for mercy because Israel is so small. In His righteousness and mercy, the Almighty gives a positive response to His servant. The LORD relents, once again displaying to the prophet His attributes of longsuffering and patience. Judgment will come because the covenant has been violated and broken. But even though the LORD is just, He is also merciful. He holds off judgment since He has no delight in the death of the sinner but that the sinner turn from his way and live (Ezekiel 18:32). The LORD's response underscores what is written in Psalm 103 and Jonah 4. The LORD is compassionate, merciful, slow to anger and abounding in steadfast love. During the course of history the LORD keeps holding back His wrath and punishment, giving us time to repent of our sins.

The first visions give us an important lesson on the power of prayer. The LORD hears the pleas and petitions of His people. He uses prayer as a means by which His plan and purpose is accomplished. "The effective, fervent prayer of a righteous man avails much" (James 5:16).

The third vision is that of a plumb line. Amos sees the LORD standing by a wall with a plumb line. A plumb line was the same as a contractor's level used to make sure things were lined up perfectly straight.

The atmosphere of this third vision is one of determination. The LORD is like a construction foreman or building inspector checking to see if the work measures up to acceptable standards. Just as a foreman must give orders to redo something that was not done right the first time so the LORD announces the destruction of Israel's religious practices. They are not true to plumb because their actions do not meet God's standards. The places of worship that are buzzing with activity must be broken down. The punishment will also touch the royal family. The LORD's judgment will come upon the house of

Jeroboam, "Behold, I am setting a plumb line in the midst of my people Israel; I will not pass by them anymore. The high places of Isaac shall be desolate, and the sanctuaries of Israel shall be laid waste. I will rise with the sword against the house of Jeroboam" (7:8,9).

The LORD uses the plumb line as an image to indicate how He measures His people. The law, testimony and ordinances of the LORD are the standard (plumb line) whereby He examines whether *we* are living true to plumb. The law – read, preached, and explained, places before us God's plumb line. It is our communal and individual responsibility to see to it that our life lines up with the plumbline. A believer's life is not true to plumb by mere outward acts but when his heart is right before the LORD, when he seeks his life in the Messiah. We depend upon the righteousness of Jesus Christ who makes our way straight.

By the time Amos explains the third vision, Amaziah the priest has had about all he can handle. He is not going to let this man from the south spoil what is going on in Bethel or let the Northern kingdom feel guilty. Amaziah resolves to put an end to this nonsense.

Amaziah sends a message to Jeroboam II which reads as follows, "Amos has conspired against you in the midst of the house of Israel; the land is not able to bear all his words. For thus Amos has said: 'Jeroboam shall die by the sword, and Israel shall surely be led away captive from their own land.'"

The priest, Amaziah, acknowledges the power of the message, for he states that the land cannot bear the words that are spoken. In his complaint Amaziah accuses Amos of being a threat to national safety by stirring up the people against the king. According to Amaziah, Amos is trying to "put more words" into the land than it can handle.

Did you notice how Amaziah misrepresents the prophet in his report to the king? His accusation is unfounded. First, he says, "Thus Amos has said..." Obviously Amaziah had not heard with the ear of faith what Amos had said. For the prophet disclosed the visions he had received to underline the fact that the words he had spoken came from the LORD. Amos did not set out on his own mission but he came to the Northern kingdom as an ambassador of the LORD. His message is peppered with, "Thus says the LORD." But Amaziah the priest conveniently ignores this and makes it a personal matter: "Amos is saying."

The second way in which Amaziah's complaint to the king misrepresents Amos lies in the fact that what he reports is incomplete. He conveys only a portion of Amos' message: the announcement of punishment. He echoes what Amos predicted (5:5). However, nothing is said about the accusations of the prophet which provide the reason why judgment is coming.

Throughout history people have used the same tactic. Servants of the LORD are often driven off course by confrontation. Their opponents may come across as being genuine and sincere. Nevertheless, they are ruthless in attacking the messenger with their criticism. To gain an audience with others and to get their point across they may conveniently leave out parts of what was said to bolster their point. When the Word of the LORD is brought in its fulness, those who are offended by it will try to diminish its seriousness by putting the messenger in a bad light in order to divert the attention away from the message.

If we are not completely open to hearing God's Word, if we have become rather full of ourselves and our own righteousness, we will find excuses to cover up why we do not want to listen to the preaching. Our Lord Jesus Christ discovered the same thing. The Jewish leaders hated His attack on their self-styled worship and therefore, they denounced Him as a political threat. They tried to nullify the message by denouncing the messenger.

Not everyone will receive the Word with joy. The Word cuts two ways: it brings joy to those who seek their salvation in Christ the Lord, but provokes opposition from those who are not prepared to take the consequences of being a follower of Christ. The worst opposition often comes from those who have deviated from Scripture and who have drawn up their own pattern for Christian piety. That is why Amaziah reacts the way he does. The truth hurts.

THE ADVICE OF THE PRIEST (12-13)

Amaziah the priest makes his complaint known to the king. While he waits for an answer, he proceeds to give his own piece of advice to the prophet of Tekoa, "Go, you seer! Flee to the land of Judah. There eat bread, and there prophesy. But never again prophesy at Bethel, for it is the king's sanctuary, and it is the royal residence."

Amaziah the priest considers the worship at Bethel to be strictly a national affair. Bethel is not considered to be the house of the LORD but the king's sanctuary and the temple of the kingdom. In Israel, the king, rather than the LORD God, determines the religious affairs of the nation (1 Kings 16:25,26,30-33; 22:52-54).

Amaziah the priest wants to silence the voice of true prophecy in the land where *he*, by the king's authority, holds the position of minister of religious affairs. Amos should stay in his own territory. By repeating the word "there" in verse 12, Amaziah makes his point quite clear. "Go eat your bread there and prophesy there and stay out of my hair," so to speak.

When the LORD prescribed how Israel was to worship Him it was clear that everyone, including the king, priests and prophets, had to submit themselves to the authority of God's word. The people did not regulate worship or religious life but the LORD did. In the Northern kingdom of Israel everything is turned upside down. Worship is made to bow before the wishes of the man in power. Jeroboam and his minister, Amaziah, will decide who will prophesy and who will not. Religion had become man-centred. The prophets need the king's permission to preach. Since Amos' message does not fit into the pattern of thinking of the Northern kingdom, he is not welcome. Israel has become accustomed to listening to prophets who were nothing but yes-men, who spoke only soothing words of comfort and gave the people what they wanted to hear (Limburg p. 117).

Amos received permission and an obligation from the King of kings to preach and prophesy but that does not seem to count in Samaria. Bethel has room only for prophets who fall in line with the state religion – as if a messenger of the LORD needs human approval or permission to speak the Word of the LORD.

Amaziah advises Amos, "Do not preach in Bethel but go back to Judah." His reaction is typical of false religion and of those who wish to serve the LORD in their own manner. The same advice has been given throughout the ages and is still given today. People want preachers who will tickle their ears with a message that pleases them. Nevertheless, the LORD warns against this type of preaching in Jeremiah 23:16,17, "Do not listen to the words of the prophets who prophesy to you. They make you worthless; they speak a vision of their own heart, not from the mouth of the LORD. They continually say to those who despise Me, 'The LORD has said, "You shall have peace'" And to everyone who walks according to the dictates of his own heart, they say, 'No evil shall come upon you.'"

The Word of God has power and demands obedience, irrespective of where we are and with whom we are talking. Politics, economics, social life and entertainment are not governed by a set of norms different from those believed and confessed in the church. Life is a unity. The same message which is proclaimed in the assembly of believers on the Lord's Day must be proclaimed and broadcasted wherever we are during the week. We may not say as Amaziah did, "Go, prophesy there but not here." The Word of the LORD is to govern how we do business, our economic transactions, social events, how we plant and sow our crops and how we do our work each day.

THE ANSWER OF THE PROPHET (14,15)

True prophets do not speak unless they have listened first. They stand in the counsel of the LORD and follow His instruction. Amos makes that clear in the answer which he gives Amaziah.

In verse 14, Amos counters Amaziah's advice with a remarkable statement, "I was no prophet, nor was I a son of a prophet, but I was a sheepbreeder and a tender of sycamore fruit. Then the LORD took me as I followed the flock, and the LORD said to me, 'Go, prophesy to my people Israel.'" Amos contrasts himself with Amaziah. He essentially says, "Amaziah, by your own declaration, you are a puppet of other human beings. You declared that the temple and sanctuary belong to the king. You are more concerned about following his whims and wishes. But I am not that kind of office-bearer! I will not say what you want to hear or be manipulated and controlled by strong and powerful individuals, but I will follow the direction of my God and King and say what you need to hear."

In response to Amaziah's command to go south and earn a living there, Amos makes the point that he was not a paid professional and he was never part of a prophetic guild. Amos says, "I was no prophet or one of the sons of the prophets." He was not one of those religious professionals who gets paid to make pious pronouncements at public occasions which do nothing more than please those who have hired them.

Amos became a prophet by the LORD's direct choosing. Similar to King David, Amos had been called from tending the sheep to fulfil his divine calling. Amaziah fails to recognize Amos' calling and mission. This is a serious matter. Refusing those who are emissaries of another is equivalent to refusing the person who sent them. As our Lord Jesus Christ would later say, "He who receives you receives Me, and he who receives Me receives Him who sent Me. He who receives a prophet in the name of a prophet shall receive a prophet's reward." (Matthew 10:40,41).

Amos tells Amaziah where his devotion as a messenger of God lies! He does not preach to please people but to be faithful to his sender. The prophet speaks as a faithful witness, declaring what the LORD has shown him (7:1,4,7). He is not telling them fanciful stories of judgment which come from his own imagination, but he proclaims what he saw. Amos will not say what the people want to hear, but what he is called to say. He will speak on the LORD's behalf uttering the words God has put in his mouth.

The Sovereign LORD had sent Amos and said, "Go, prophesy to my people." Amos did not go to the Northern kingdom to meddle in the affairs of others. He was sent because the LORD loves His people. In His compassion, grace and mercy He calls them to return. And so, when the LORD calls prophets and ministers to preach they may not move aside for anyone.

In the office of all believers we are called to speak in Christ's name. Everything we say must show our love and devotion for the LORD and for the cause of His kingdom. We should not worry that what we say might damage our relationship with our family or that it may cost us our job. The church, the assembly of God's covenant people, is the LORD's sanctuary! Therefore we should not shy away from speaking the truth of the gospel.

As children of the LORD we should never cave in and bow to the pressure of those who take the seats of power and want to be in control. May we never hesitate to speak what the LORD wants us to say, even if it offends our best friend. In true love for fellow humans the greater act of kindness is to admonish a person for his disobedience so that he may turn to the LORD and live.

THE PUNISHMENT OF THE LORD (16, 17)

In the Northern kingdom of Israel the people sacrificed, prayed and celebrated but God shows them that they lack one thing. They have not given themselves to the LORD with a total commitment of their heart. Therefore, the LORD will certainly judge and punish those who serve Him in their own manner. Through His emissary, the LORD says to the self-styled priest of Bethel, "You say, 'Do not prophesy against Israel, and do not spout against the house of Isaac.' Therefore thus says the LORD: 'your wife shall be a harlot in the city; your sons and daughters shall fall by the sword; your land shall be divided by survey line; you shall die in a defiled land; and Israel shall surely be led away captive from his own land.'"

The priesthood of Amaziah will be publicly disgraced. His wife will openly engage in prostitution to provide for herself. His children will be killed. The land in which Israel placed their security will be taken away from Amaziah and his family.

Here we have another indication of how self-willed Israel had become in their worship of God. Strikingly, Amaziah, a priest, will also be dispossessed of his land! According to the law, the priests who served in God's sanctuary were not supposed to have their own land. The LORD had said to Aaron, "You shall have no inheritance in their land, nor shall you have any portion among them; I am your portion and your inheritance among the children of Israel" (Number 18:20).

The LORD will not be mocked! The most terrible things will happen. Amaziah and his family will die in an *unclean* land. What a horrible punishment! That is equivalent to saying Amaziah will die excommunicated from the LORD and His people. He will be set outside the land of the covenant.

Our God never leaves sin unpunished. He deals swiftly with those who threaten His prophets (Jeremiah 11:18-23) or persecute them (Jeremiah 20:6). This is true for us as well. The LORD will not leave sin unpunished but He has punished it through the atoning sacrifice of His only begotten Son. It is a wonder of God's grace that we may continue with Him. Let us humble ourselves before the LORD and seek our well-being in our only Mediator Jesus Christ. He is the focal point of our religion, our worship and our life. In Christ, our ears are made receptive to the Word.

As faithful followers of our Lord Jesus Christ may we be eager and diligent to hear God's Word. Let it be our constant prayer, "Speak LORD for Your servant hears. My ears are open to your wisdom and instruction. I know Your words are the words of life because they direct me to Him who is the Way, the Truth and the Life and who fulfilled all righteousness for me through a sacrifice which was true to plumb. In Him I know of Your mercy because He took upon Himself my sin and the punishment I deserve." With the Scriptures in hand may we, as prophets, proclaim the Name of the LORD as it has been revealed to us.

Questions

1. The first six chapters of this prophecy have shown how the people of the Northern kingdom of Israel are religious but not obedient. Explain what this means. How do we still see that happening in our own contemporary setting?

2. What role do visions play in the last three chapters of the prophecy of Amos?

3. Look up Jeremiah 1:11-19 and Jeremiah 24:1-10. What are some of the similarities in structure, formulas, content and message between Jeremiahs's three visions and the five Amos received?

4. Why does Amos intercede for the people in the first and second vision? In both cases the LORD hears the petition of His servant and calls off what He was planning to do. How do these verses encourage us in our intercessory prayers?

5. What is meant by the expression "the king's mowings" (verse 1)? What is the significance of the fact that the locusts appeared after the king's mowings?

6. Does verse 3 suggest that if we beseech the LORD unceasingly that we can pray a problem away? Explain your answer by comparing this text to other parts of Scripture which speak about prayer.

7. What is the message of the first three visions (7:1-9)? What does the metaphor of a plumb line teach us?

8. Why does the encounter between true and false leadership interrupt the revelation of the five visions?

9. Why does Amaziah tell Amos to leave Israel and to prophesy in Judah instead?

10. When there is a disagreement, people will make their criticism personal. Give examples of how this has happened in history. How can such a recourse be avoided?

11. The kings of Israel were highly influential in the religious affairs of the Northern kingdom. Give examples of times when this has happened again in church history. Should we conclude that church and state should always be separate?

12. What was the significance of land for the people of the LORD in the Old Testament? How was this tied to the promise of the coming Messiah? Amaziah was to be dispossessed of his land. Why was he not supposed to possess land in the first place?

CHAPTER 11

THE LORD TAKES AWAY HIS WORD FROM THOSE WHO WILL NOT HEAR IT

Reading: Deut 30:9-20; Amos 8:1-10
Song Selection: Psalms 43,65,73,147

Key verses: Amos 8:11-12
"Behold, the days are coming," says the LORD *GOD,*
"That I will send a famine on the land,
Not a famine of bread,
Nor a thirst for water,
But of hearing the words of the LORD.
They shall wander from sea to sea,
And from north to east;
They shall run to and fro, seeking the word of the LORD,
But shall not find it."

Throughout the prophecy of Amos, the LORD gives ample examples of how the people of the Northern kingdom of Israel are not as religious and God-fearing as they may think. They

125

are very busy with the rituals of worship, thinking this is sanctioned by the LORD, yet the Almighty God is not at all pleased. Their religiosity will only bring burning coals of fire on their heads as long as they do not repent.

The people go through the rituals of worship but in the meantime they cannot get their minds off their work. In chapter 8: 4-6, the prophet lays seven charges against the people and all of them have to do with how they do business and what effect this has on others within the communion of saints. *Outwardly*, Israel is doing just fine. They are careful to observe the feast days prescribed by the LORD, shutting their shops on the Sabbath day and on other religious feast days. Although their shops are closed, their minds are open to the concerns of their businesses, which would be operating at full tilt the minute the Sabbath ends. They can hardly wait until the Sabbath is over so that they can again go about their daily business of getting gain for themselves. Whatever they do is not meant to help others who are in need. By their ruthless greed they seek their own gain and in effect exterminate the needy. In fact, they take advantage of others by cheating and being dishonest. More than likely they would not have considered themselves devious or ungodly in these matters.

Once again the LORD reminds us that true religion not only has to do with the Sabbath and with the sanctuary, but also with shops and the shekel. How we go to work and spend our money must be determined by what we receive on the Sabbath in the sanctuary. Living for the LORD and for each other in the communion of saints is a full-time job and a life-long commitment.

We may wonder: why do people lose touch with the guidelines of covenant living? Why was it that people started acting the way they did in the Northern kingdom? This happens when the Word of the LORD does not receive a central place in our life. There could come a time when the LORD will take away from us the very Word He has given us for our guidance.

THE SIGNIFICANCE OF WHAT THE LORD IS DOING

Before the people of Israel had entered into Canaan, the LORD admonished them to keep themselves to the simplicity of His Word.

The LORD warned them not to start looking for His testimonies and precepts in places where they would not find them. Through His servant Moses the LORD impressed upon the hearts of His people how they were to serve Him with all their heart, soul and strength. They are a covenant people whose worship and daily conduct is to be governed by the living Word of the LORD.

As God's people we are to listen carefully to the voice of the living God as He addresses us through His servants. In Deuteronomy 4:2 we read, "You shall not add to the word which I command you, nor take from it, that you may keep the commandments of the LORD your God which I command you."

The LORD had brought Israel into the wilderness to teach them to live by His Word. Thus Moses says in Deuteronomy 8:3, "So He humbled you, allowed you to hunger, and fed you with manna which you did not know nor did your fathers know, that He might make you know that man shall not live by bread alone; but man lives by every word that proceeds from the mouth of the LORD."

The nearness of God's Word is the guarantee of Israel's continued existence as covenant people of the LORD. This is what Deuteronomy 30:11-14 assures us of, "For this commandment which I command you today is not too mysterious for you, nor is it far off. It is not in heaven, that you should say, 'Who will ascend into heaven for us and bring it to us, that we may hear it and do it?' Nor is it beyond the sea, that you should say, 'Who will go over the sea for us and bring it to us, that we may hear it and do it?' But the word is very near you, in your mouth and in your heart, that you may do it."

What is stated in Deuteronomy 30 is a fundamental rule of the covenant. The LORD establishes a relationship with His children and He speaks to them in a manner easily understood. Yet when Amos came to preach and prophesy to the Northern kingdom, he addressed a people who only listened to the Word of the LORD when it suited them. But how does the LORD react to that? Does he pass it off as "no big deal?" Absolutely not! God's people conveniently put off and blocked out of their minds what the LORD required of them. Nevertheless, God will never forget what they do that is contrary to His will. One day they will have to answer for the wrongs they have done before Him. Chapter 8:7 & 10 reads, "The LORD has sworn by the pride of Jacob: 'Surely I will never forget any of their works... I will turn your feasts into mourning, and all your songs into lamentation...'"

A vision Amos receives from the LORD makes this point. We read of it in chapter 8:1-3. Israel is like a piece of fruit which looks beautiful and inviting on the outside but is bruised and rotten on the inside. They are fit to be thrown away – out of the land of promise.

Thus the Sovereign LORD declares, "'Behold, the days are coming,' says the LORD God, 'That I will send a famine on the land, not a famine of bread, nor a thirst for water, but of hearing the words of the LORD'" (verse 11).

Amos, as a farmer from Tekoa, knew exactly what the LORD was talking about when He spoke of judgment in terms of famine, drought and plague. The LORD will take away the bread of life and the food which nourishes their souls to everlasting life. He will call back all His prophets and shut the heavens so that in the North country it will become very, very silent. They will no longer hear the promises of the gospel concerning salvation in the coming Messiah. The people of the covenant will be deprived of all comfort when in distress. All instruction, correction and hope are taken from them.

For a long time the people of Israel refused to listen completely to the Word. They did not have the Word as the focal point of their life. The warning cry of God's servants, the prophets, fell on deaf ears. The message proclaimed to them as they assembled on the Sabbath went right by them because their minds were busy with other things. Their busy schedules were tiring them out so they had little patience to sit and listen to the Word of the LORD. The people were not all that interested in what the prophet Amos had to say to them either. They did not want him telling them what they were supposed to be doing or what they were to refrain from doing. They complained, "Amos is always so hard on us. He's so negative about what we are doing in the North. Why doesn't he go back home and stay out of our territory?"

In chapter 7 Amaziah, a priest at Bethel, verbalized what the people thought about true prophecy. He told Amos in no uncertain terms that he should pack up his bags and leave!

Israel did not want to hear the true Word of the LORD so now the LORD says to them, "You're not going to get it either."At one time the Word was *near* them but when the LORD sends a famine of hearing His Word they will search high and low, but they will not find it. "Behold, the days are coming, says the LORD God."

What the LORD said through Amos to the Northern kingdom was not only meant for them but is a powerful message for the church of all ages and places. If the Word of the LORD does not take central place in our lives, the LORD may take away from us the privilege of hearing it. And so we all have to evaluate how we listen. Is the Word, which is near us now in the preaching, the focal point of our life? How well do we listen to what is being said and how serious are we about applying the standard of Scripture to what we do?

Christianity is much more than a private matter. It is a worldview. Being busy with the Word of the LORD involves more than showing up for two hours of worship on the Lord's Day. It must permeate our thinking and leave its signature on all our actions. That means we should make time, especially on the Lord's Day, for personal and family devotions and congregational Bible Study. Frequently things get turned around. Our work, our earthly cares and concerns are given a higher priority than the study of God's Word or advancing the ministry of the gospel in the congregation.

Spiritual malnutrition is a major problem besetting modern Christianity. The effects are deadly. Undernourishment is not due to a lack of resources, but to a loss of desire to use them. Many in the church suffer malnutrition because they do not want to eat. They do not hunger for it.

Next to our coming together on the Lord's Day, studying the Word of the LORD together as congregation is a very important way of getting to know each other. We have a responsibility to be busy with the Word of God together and in this way to fulfil our calling to live for each other. As congregation we are not to neglect meeting together, to study and encourage each other with the Word of the LORD and all the more as the day of Christ's return draws near (Hebrews 10:25). The same principle applies here as in giving of our first fruits. If we do not give to the LORD *first*, we probably will not receive anything.

In Amos' time, the LORD's people were trampling upon the needs of the poor and did not care about others because they had lost touch with the Word that was near them. Therefore their own deeds will condemn them. The LORD will bring upon them spiritual poverty. If we are not careful to follow the Word of the LORD, He will strike us with a famine of the Word and we will not find comfort in time of need.

You may have a reputation for being a hard worker; you may throw everything into making the business you are involved in prosper, but what good is that if you do not feed yourself with spiritual food? If you refuse to eat of the bread of life when it is set before you, the LORD will take it from you and give it to another.

THE EFFECTS OF WHAT THE LORD IS DOING

Amos vividly describes the effects of the spiritual famine in verse 12, "They shall wander from sea to sea, and from north to east; they shall run to and fro seeking the word of the LORD, but shall not find it." The picture is of a man out in the desert dying of hunger and thirst. He wanders back and forth. Faint with thirst he looks for water. Gradually, his strength diminishes. He begins to stagger and fall. Finally he cannot get up anymore.

The Northern kingdom of Israel will hunger for comfort and consolation but they will not find it. They stagger from sea to sea, that is, from the one boundary of the inheritance God has given to them to the other; they go from North to East. They look to the religion of Assyria and to the culture of Babylon for consolation and comfort but they will not find any. Strikingly, they do not search for it in the South, in the land of Judah where it can still be found.

The famine of hearing the Word affects the children, too. "In that day the fair virgins and strong young men shall faint from thirst" (v.13). The children have not learned from their parents to bend in submission to the authority of the Word of the LORD. They haven't been taught to fight against world conformity. The false prophets have lulled them to sleep. All they have seen is parents who are more concerned with material goods than with spiritual enrichment. The children see adults who are not busy with God's

Word in their every day life, who do not practice what is preached, but who are occupied with all sorts of other things. Therefore they will be affected by the famine, too. They will have a thirst for answers to the problems and difficulties of life, but that thirst will not be quenched. The famine of hearing the Word will impoverish their lives and rob them of all their energy and inner strength. They search for the truth but they will not find it.

We observe such a famine in our own times too. When people do not listen to the Word of the LORD and do not use the opportunities the LORD gives then it does not take long before they find the sermons which deal with all the aspects of God's counsel too difficult. They have trouble talking to other church members or to their own children about what is preached. Life becomes increasingly shallow. Such things as entertainment and sports have a higher priority than Bible study and developing a Christian lifestyle. People become satisfied with a cheap interpretation of Scripture as they look for preachers who make for easy listening.

The LORD showed Israel that He meant what He said. Shortly after Amos prophesied these words, the Northern kingdom is sent into captivity. And there is no prophet who accompanied them into Assyria or who spoke to them afterward. The people may hunger to hear the comfort of the LORD but there is no one to console them.

There is a famine of hearing the words of the LORD for years! Christ is the next prophet to step into Samaria. He ends the drought. That adds a whole new dimension to the conversation Christ had with the woman of Samaria at Jacob's well! What does Christ speak about? Drinking from the living waters! When a person drinks of this water he will never thirst again. The Word made flesh puts an end to the famine through His own work and through that of His apostles.

After Pentecost Christ sends His apostles out to be His witnesses in Jerusalem, Judea and Samaria...(Acts 1:8). The famine is ended when the Word of the LORD comes from the South! The Samaritans, who form what remains of the Northern kingdom, do not seek the Word but God seeks them out. The Word comes to them through the apostles.

God will send a famine of hearing the words of the LORD when His people reject true prophecy. Can that happen to us? Amos 8 shows that it can! On the other hand, when our hearts are completely open to hearing the Word of the LORD, He will bless us and feed us with the bread of life. Today there is no excuse to be faint with thirst or to be sick with hunger. Did Christ not say, "...he who comes to Me shall never hunger, and he who believes in Me shall never thirst." (John 6:35)? The people of the LORD who hear and respond in faith will be fed with plenty.

The Word of God is near us. We hear it every Lord's Day. We have the opportunity to study it. Let us be busy with the Word to the day when the whole earth, from sea to sea, from east to west and from north to south, will be filled with the knowledge of the Word of the LORD!

Questions

1. How does a basket of summer fruit symbolize the destruction of the people of Israel? What is the reason why destruction is coming?

2. Psalm 92 is a psalm for the Sabbath. How does this psalm show us the foundation and character of proper Sabbath worship? How does this psalm keep us from a wrong way of looking at the Sabbath day?

3. The Heidelberg Catechism, in Lord's Day 38, states that we are to diligently attend the church of God especially (not exclusively) on the Sabbath day. What does this tell us about the relationship between the Lord's Day and the other days of the week?

4. The stress and busyness of life threaten family life and have taken their toll on a proper functioning of the communion of saints. Those who have special needs (e.g., single, widows and orphans) are not always given the care they need. How does this busyness threaten our Sabbath rest? Think of what it did to Amos' contemporaries.

5. Throughout the prophecy of Amos, the LORD speaks of "the pride of Jacob." What is meant by this expression (see 8:7 and 6:8)?

6. What is the symbolic meaning of the "sun going down at noon" and "darkening the earth at noon" (compare verse 9 with Deut 28:29 and Jeremiah 15:8,9)?

7. Why will the LORD bring baldness upon every head (verse 10)? What does this signify?

8. What kind of famine are the verses 11-14 speaking about? Has such a famine been experienced at other times in history? How does this famine affect the children of the covenant?

9. Does the famine of the Word only mean a physical removal of the prophets from the people or can it also mean more? Can it also refer to a spiritual inability to absorb the message of God's Word through a hardening of the heart? (See further Isaiah 6:9,10; Matthew 13:13-17)

10. Turn to 2 Corinthians 3:14-18. What is the parallel between this passage and Amos 8:11-12?

11. What kind of problems arise when people think the Word of the LORD no longer speaks to their circumstances?

12. Why do the people of the Northern kingdom of Israel refuse to seek the Word of the LORD in the south? Does that tell us something about the nature of sin and pride?

13. Read John 4. How does the conversation of Jesus with the woman at the well of Samaria indicate that the LORD, in His mercy, breaks the spiritual drought in Samaria?

14. What is the sin (shame) of Samaria (verse 14)?

CHAPTER 12

THE LORD WARNS HIS PEOPLE, "YOU CAN RUN BUT YOU CANNOT HIDE!"

Reading: Psalm 139
Song Selection: Psalms 27,32,46,119,139

Key verses: Amos 9:1-6
I saw the LORD *standing by the altar, and He said:*
"Strike the doorposts, that the thresholds may shake,
And break them on the heads of them all.
I will slay the last of them with the sword.
He who flees from them shall not get away,
And he who escapes from them shall not be delivered.

"Though they dig into hell,
From there My hand shall take them;
Though they climb up to heaven,
From there I will bring them down;
And though they hide themselves on top of Carmel,
From there I will search and take them;
Though they hide from My sight at the bottom of the sea,

From there I will command the serpent,
and it shall bite them;
Though they go into captivity before their enemies,
From there I will command the sword,
And it shall slay them.
I will set My eyes on them for harm and not for good."
The LORD *God of hosts,*
He who touches the earth and it melts,
And all who dwell there mourn;
All of it shall swell like the River,
And subside like the River of Egypt.
He who builds His layers in the sky,
And has founded His strata in the earth;
Who calls for the waters of the sea,
And pours them out on the face of the earth –
The LORD *is His name.*

*W*e turn our attention to the last of Amos' five visions. As was mentioned previously, these visions demonstrate a clear progression from bad to worse. In the first two visions, the swarm of locusts and the fire, Amos entreats the LORD and prays that God might defer His judgment. Both times the LORD yields and declares it will not happen. But in the following three visions, the plumb line (7:7-9), the basket of summer fruit (8:1-3) and the destruction of the altar (9:1-4), the judgment of the LORD is irreversible and final.

These five visions are like a picture confirming that what Amos has been proclaiming is not his own opinion but has been revealed to him by the LORD. The downfall of the people is certain because they do not listen to the Word of the LORD. The Israelites are very busy performing all sorts of religious rituals and are not worried in the least about the day of the LORD. Yet the LORD warns them that they will be punished and will go into exile because they have constructed their own pattern of worship.

The last vision is somewhat different from the previous four in that the LORD Himself reports it. What He states is most unsettling.

The LORD is seen standing by the altar, speaking words of judgment against His people. He will tear down their self-designed sanctuaries of worship because the only place of refuge is in the ministry of reconciliation that points to salvation in Christ alone.

There are other visions in Scripture in which the LORD is pictured *seated* in council. For example, the prophet Micaiah says to king Ahab, "I saw the LORD sitting on His throne, and all the host of heaven standing by, on His right hand and on His left..."(1 Kings 22:19). Isaiah saw the LORD sitting upon a throne, high and lifted up with the seraphim standing above Him (6:1,2). The fact that the LORD is standing beside the altar is significant. In the ancient world a king would *sit* when he was in council but he would *stand* when he delivered his sentence and judgment. The LORD describes Himself as the Sovereign LORD, who builds up *and* tears down. For one last time the LORD confronts His people with what is coming. This time He declares His judgment by emphasizing who He is.

THERE IS NO HIDING FROM GOD (1-4)

In this fifth vision Amos sees the LORD suddenly coming to His people. He meets them at the heart of their religious ceremonies and worship. The people have gathered together in a sanctuary which *they* have erected for worship. The sanctuary is full of people who perform rituals and religious formalities. There is much singing and sacrificing going on. Everyone is happy and feeling good about how they are worshipping the LORD.

God wanted the altar to be at the centre of Israel's worship. At the altar the worshipper received assurance of mercy and forgiveness through atonement. The purpose of everything that went on in the sanctuary was to proclaim the name of the LORD, and it foreshadowed the redemption the Messiah would obtain for His people. Under the wings of God's mercy a believer found a hiding place! This is why David said in Psalm 27, "One thing I have desired of the LORD, that will I seek: that I may dwell in the house of the LORD all the days of my life, to behold the beauty of the LORD, and to inquire in His temple. For in the time of trouble He shall hide me in His pavilion; in the secret place of His tabernacle He shall hide me; He shall set me high upon a rock."

From the very place where the people expected to hear words of peace and blessing the LORD pronounces destruction. He does not stand by the altar to approve what transpires nor to offer shelter but to condemn the altar, the sanctuary and the worshippers. The Almighty pronounces His sentence. The altar Israel has erected is not in the designated place the LORD had chosen. Therefore He gives orders that this place of self-willed religion be broken into pieces, "Strike the doorposts, that the thresholds may shake, and break them on the heads of them all. I will slay the last of them with the sword. He who flees from them shall not get away."

The LORD condemns what is happening in the sanctuary. This is no place to feel secure because the sacrifices being offered are worthless. The practices both within and outside the sanctuary betray what kind of people Israel has become. They have rejected God's covenant ordinances and designed their own standards for living. As long as they do not repent they will not find refuge in the LORD. The sanctuary will not be a hiding place.

The LORD commands the one who is to execute His judgment, "Strike the doorposts, that the thresholds may shake." The doorposts, or better translated, "capitals," were the rounded parts on the top of the ornamental columns which supported the sanctuary's roof. If the capitals were struck, the beams of the foundation would shake and the whole structure would crumble. Thus the LORD steps in and disrupts the activity of the people. No one will escape His wrath. The sword will find those who escape the destruction of the temple. There will be no survivors.

Even though the Israelites formally worshipped God with a great deal of outward piety, their deeds expose what really lives in their hearts and how far they have wandered away from the truth. In utter foolishness they think that somehow they can escape from being under the watchful eye of the LORD. They act like little children who put their hands in front of their own eyes and believe that no one can see them.

The people of the Northern kingdom of Israel thought they could escape the judgment of the LORD through death. But the LORD tells His people to forget that idea. "Though they dig into hell, from there My hand shall take them."

In Scripture, Sheol (translated by the NKJV as hell) refers to the realm of the dead. It is the place where both the righteous and the wicked are laid to rest. Nevertheless, those who die are not out of the LORD's reach.

Sheol and heaven occur more often in parallel to indicate the extent of the LORD's rule and authority. For example Zophar says to Job in chapter 11:7,8, "Can you search out the deep things of God? Can you find out the limits of the Almighty? They are higher than heaven – what can you do? Deeper than Sheol – what can you know? Their measure is longer than the earth and broader than the sea."

Amos 9:2-4 also indicates how the people of Israel were influenced by the surrounding cultures which drew them further away from the LORD through their practices. The cultures of Babylon and Assyria placed great emphasis on the study of the heavens. Similar to the philosophy of our day, they saw their life connected to the world of spirits and to the "energies" and "biorhythms" in the universe. The people of the Northern kingdom of Israel were affected by the Canaanite culture which put great stock in the fertility rites that went along with the worship of Baal. They were also influenced by the culture of Egypt which spoke of great sea monsters controlling the depths of the sea and offering people protection and safety.

It is also noteworthy that Carmel is mentioned specifically as a place where the people will try to find refuge. Mount Carmel was densely forested at the top, providing many hiding places. The top of Carmel was also the place where the LORD had made a clear statement of His sovereignty and holiness. The LORD will not share His glory with the idols. He will not tolerate any form of syncretic religion. The prophet says the people will not be able to hide or escape the wrath of the LORD in this place of redemptive-historical significance. Its physical terrain will not lend any protection either.

The LORD warns His people of their folly. There is nothing that can hide them from God's presence. They cannot escape judgment no matter how hard they try or where they flee. Man can go nowhere beyond the government of God. "Though they climb up to heaven, from there I will bring them down" (9:2). There is no place to run and no place to hide when the living God comes to judge the deeds of His people. All creation is subject to the LORD and will assist Him in punishing the wicked (see further Hosea 10:6-8; Luke 23:30; Revelation 6:16).

The LORD takes away every possibility of escape. It will not be found in exile either. To this point Amos had presented captivity and exile as being the worst thing that could happen to the Northern kingdom. They will be driven out of the land of the inheritance and away from the land of promise. The people will be removed from their homeland, separated from many of their loved ones, and forced to live in near solitude for many years. But now Amos warns that even in exile they should not think they are separated from the LORD. God's power is not limited to the land of Canaan. His judgment is executed over all the earth.

The effect of God's presence is quite the opposite of what we read in other parts of scripture. Take what David confesses in Psalm 139:7-12, "Where can I go from Your Spirit? Or where can I flee from Your presence? If I ascend into heaven, You are there; If I make my bed in hell, behold, You are there. If I take the wings of the morning, and dwell in the uttermost parts of the sea, even there Your hand shall lead me, and Your right hand shall hold me. If I say, 'Surely the darkness shall fall on me,' even the night shall be light about me; indeed, the darkness shall not hide from You, but the night shines as the day; the darkness and the light are both alike to You."

Both Amos and David speak of God's omnipresence. The very same attribute of God is a source of great joy, blessing and hope to the believer but spells nothing but doom for those who live in sin and disobedience. In Psalm 139 David expresses his amazement and his awe that no matter where he is the LORD is present with him. But in Amos 9 that same attribute ought to evoke a sense of fear and terror. As we read in verse 8, "Behold, the eyes of the LORD GOD are on the sinful kingdom, and I will destroy it from the face of the earth..."

The LORD's eyes are upon His creatures and He sees all their actions. That is comforting to the believer who knows nothing can separate him from the love of God in Christ Jesus. But God's omnipresence condemns those who live in sin. Our sins are not hidden from the LORD. We cannot withdraw ourselves from the presence of the LORD or hide behind our innocence or ignorance. It happens in our times that individuals who are confronted with their sins and are placed under the discipline of the church, think they can withdraw themselves from the service of the LORD and His people and thereby escape the LORD's judgment of excommunication. But what they are doing is fooling themselves. No one can escape the LORD's judgment on sin.

No matter where we go or what we do it is all known to the LORD. The LORD knows what we are doing in the secret hiding places we may have. He hears what we are whispering and sees what we do at work, at home or wherever we may be. There is nothing hidden which will not be revealed. "For the eyes of the LORD run to and fro throughout the whole earth, to show Himself strong on behalf of those whose heart is loyal to Him" (2 Chronicles 16:9). This is to our comfort when we seek our life in Christ. Yet where there is no true faith or acceptance of all that the LORD has revealed to us in His Word there is no escape. " 'Can anyone hide himself in secret places, so I shall not see him?' says the LORD; 'Do I not fill heaven and earth?' says the LORD" (Jeremiah 23:24). "And there is no creature hidden from His sight, but all things are naked and open to the eyes of Him to whom we must give account" (Hebrews 4:13). We may run but we cannot hide from the living God. "The LORD is in His holy temple, the LORD's throne is in heaven; His eyes behold, His eyelids test the sons of men" (Psalm 11:4). Furthermore, when we walk by faith we will not want to run because in Him we have a hiding place.

THERE IS A HIDING PLACE IN GOD (5-6)

At first reading, verses 5 and 6 may seem disconnected from the first four verses. Amos says, "The LORD GOD of hosts, He who touches the earth and it melts, and all who dwell there mourn; all of it shall swell like the River, and subside like the River of Egypt. He who builds His layers in the sky, and has founded His strata in the earth; who calls for the waters of the sea, and pours them out on the face of the earth – the LORD is His name."

The last five words, "The LORD is His name" pull these verses together! When "LORD" appears in capital letters, it signifies God's covenant name. The LORD, who comes to judge His disobedient people, is the God who established His covenant with believers and their children. He is the LORD who said to Abraham, "Do not be afraid, I am your shield" (Genesis 15:1).Those whose walk is blameless find a hiding place in the LORD. The LORD of hosts, the Sovereign Creator of heaven and earth, is the only protection of any people. The LORD who has the power to strike the earth with the fire of His judgment so that it melts before Him (2 Peter 3:10) is our only hope. Blessed are the people who find their refuge in the LORD (Psalm 2).

It is intriguing how the prophet Amos weaves the theme of God's providential care into what he has to say to this people. Amos makes this connection several times to show Israel how they have gone completely off track. He says in chapter 4:13, "For behold, He who forms mountains, and creates the wind, who declares to man what his thought is, and makes the morning darkness, who treads the high places of the earth – the LORD, the God of hosts is His name!" Chapter 5:8 says much the same, "He made the Pleiades and Orion; He turns the shadow of death into morning and makes the day dark as night; He calls for the waters of the sea and pours them out on the face of the earth; the LORD is His name."

Amos contrasts the glory of the covenant God – His majesty, splendour and power – with the degeneration of the people who know His name. When the prophet sees the people sinning so grievously, his mind turns to the LORD. Amos is disturbed that people do as they please, and trample God's covenant laws underfoot without considering what the LORD Himself might think or do about it. There is no fear of the LORD in their hearts.

As a man who would have spent many hours outdoors, Amos had an eye for the majesty of the LORD'S creation. He knew God as the builder and Creator of the world and everything in it. Amos also knew Him as the One who will continue to maintain what He has made for the sake of the covenant He established with His people. He who made the mountains, the wind and the stars, has not withdrawn Himself from His creation. His purpose is to bring complete deliverance, redemption and renewal for all creation through the work of His Son.

The One who has the forces of nature in His hand cannot be

thwarted or stopped by the sinful actions of His people. The heavy rain season in Ethiopia caused the Nile river to rise by as much as twenty-five feet, flooding the whole valley and leaving behind rich silt. But that was not some natural phenomenon. The providential hand of the LORD caused this to happen.

Through Amos the LORD appeals to His people to recognize His power both to judge and to save. The Creator of heaven and earth says in covenant love, "Be still and know, all you who bide Me, that I am God and none beside Me." He wants them to respond, "The LORD of hosts is on our side; with Jacob's God we safely hide" (Psalm 46).

When people try to hide from God they soon find out that it is impossible. He who made heaven and earth has the ability to search you out and find you no matter where you are. Adam and Eve found this out in Paradise when they tried to flee from the presence of the LORD. Jonah, the prophet, discovered it when he tried to avoid the task the LORD had given to him. David was made aware of how miserable his life became when he attempted in vain to hide from God. And now the people of the Northern kingdom are reminded of the same thing. When you sin, you may try to flee from the presence of the LORD but you cannot hide. He will find you out. No one can escape His judgment.

On the other hand, when you confess your sins and find shelter in the name of the LORD you will discover how good it is to be hidden in the LORD. True joy and peace is realized when your life is hid with God and in the atonement that was made by Christ at the altar of Golgotha. The Father stood beside the altar of Christ's cross and touched His Son with His wrath so that the very foundations and thresholds of the earth shook and trembled. Even though Jesus prayed fervently, "Let this cup pass," there was no way of escape and no place to hide.

Since our sins have been laid on the altar of Golgotha we can be assured that there is escape from the bondage and dominion of sin through Jesus Christ our Lord. Therefore, let Christ continue to be the focus of our worship and praise. Our covenant LORD, who has created the world, and who maintains it, is faithful. He will show the glory of His name in being our security and hope. We cannot hide *from* the LORD but we can hide *in* Him. With the psalmist we confess, "You are my hiding place and my shield; I hope in Your Word" (Psalm 119:114). Or to put it in the words of a familiar hymn, "Rock of ages cleft for me. Let me hide myself in thee."

Questions

1. Amos sees the LORD standing by the altar (Amos 9:1) To which altar is Amos referring? What evidence favours the altar in Bethel? Is there anything suggesting that it could be the altar at Jerusalem (1:2)?

2. Why would the LORD proclaim His judgment standing by the altar?

3. Which attribute of the LORD is highlighted in verse 2? What does this tell us about the foolishness of trying to hide sin?

4. In Psalm 139:8 God's presence in Sheol is a source of hope whereas in Amos 9:2 it spells destruction and trouble. Discuss what is said about God's presence in Sheol within the context of each passage. What does this tell us about how messages should be delivered at funerals?

5. What is the LORD saying to Israel when He says, "There I will command the serpent, and it shall bite them" (verse 3)?

6. Israel is now a "sinful kingdom." Is Israel reduced to the level or status of other nations by means of the punishments received? What was her original calling (Exodus 19:6)?

7. What is the meaning of the LORD's question in verse 7, "Are you not like the people of Ethiopia to Me...?" What does this verse say about Israel's relationship with the LORD?

8. The eyes of the LORD are on the sinful kingdom (verse 8).

The expression "eyes of the LORD" is often used to convey both God's blessing and also His curse. Look up Gen 44:21; Lev 20:3,5,6; 2 Chron 16:9; Ps 34:16; Jer 21:10; 24:6 and Ezek 15:7 to see how this is demonstrated in these passages.

9. Amos 9:8 says the Northern kingdom of Israel will be destroyed but not totally. How does this fit with chapter 9:1-4 where no one seems to escape?

10. Since Amos announced the end of the Northern kingdom of Israel as a nation, can there be any future for anyone from this region? Are there any indications in previous chapters that the LORD will preserve a remnant from the ten tribes of Israel?

CHAPTER 13

THE LORD PROMISES TO REBUILD DAVID'S HOUSE IN THE COMING OF HIS SON

Reading: Acts 1:1-11; 15:6-18
Song Selection: Psalms 21,72,85,89

Key verses: Amos 9:11-15
"On that day I will raise up
The tabernacle of David, which has fallen down,
And repair its damages;
I will raise up its ruins,
And rebuild it as in the days of old;
That they may possess the remnant of Edom,
And all the Gentiles who are called by My name,"
Says the LORD *who does this thing.*

"Behold, the days are coming," says the LORD,
"When the plowman shall overtake the reaper,
And the treader of grapes him who sows seed;
The mountains shall drip with sweet wine,
And all the hills shall flow with it.

I will bring back the captives of My people Israel;
They shall build the waste cities and inhabit them;
They shall plant vineyards and drink wine from them;
They shall also make gardens and eat fruit from them.
I will plant them in their land,
And no longer shall they be pulled up
From the land I have given them,"
Says the LORD *your God.*

The prophet Amos had the unenviable task of proclaiming a message peppered with doom, destruction and devastation. He is commissioned to tell the people of the LORD that they should not boast in their special position because the LORD will judge them just as He has pronounced His verdict on the surrounding nations. God condemns their religious complacency, their self-willed worship and their failure to practice obedience to the will of God in all spheres of life. No one will escape the wrath of the LORD. The LORD warns in the verse preceding our text, "All the sinners of My people shall die by the sword, who say, 'The calamity shall not overtake nor confront us'"(9:10). Israel will surely go into exile. The threat of being removed from the promised land struck at the very heart of Israel's relationship with God.

For the sake of His own name, the LORD cannot back down from what He said He would do. Yet, in wrath the LORD remembers mercy. The yearnings of His heart cry out to those who have strayed from the path of His covenant. He appeals to them, calling them to return to His ways. As the LORD pronounces His judgment upon those who do not repent, He also comforts a faithful remnant by repeating the promises He made of old. The LORD says, "Never!" to the thought of total destruction. He will not forsake the work of His hands. His messianic goals will not be thwarted. His undeserved favour triumphs in that He will keep for Himself a certain number of people chosen to everlasting life.

Amos ends on a positive note and with a message of grace. Yet what he says does not undo previous warnings. The people may not skip over the "bad news" to get on with the "good news." The blessings of the covenant are granted to us through faith and obedience. This is a word of comfort for a faithful remnant and not for those who continue living in sin.

The same ministry of the Word which *closes* the kingdom of heaven to the sinful kingdom of the North (which continues to march to the drum of self-willed worship) *opens* the kingdom and publishes the glorious news of forgiveness and everlasting life to those who repent of their sins. The LORD will restore the fortunes of His people by establishing the kingdom of David. Through the coming of His Son, God will mend what has been broken apart through sin.

Living in the New Dispensation we have the privilege of knowing how the Word which the LORD spoke through Amos had its fulfilment in the birth and ascension of Christ, and in the gathering of God's elect through the working of the Holy Spirit.

HOW DAVID'S HOUSE WILL BE RESTORED BY THE LORD

The major theme of the book of Amos is the plea for a return to the right worship of God which reflects a correct understanding of who God is. Israel must worship Him as He has made Himself known to them. The Northern kingdom had developed a system of worship which failed to put the LORD at the centre of all of life. Therefore Amos calls on the people to remember the LORD their God. They must return to the pattern of worship He had prescribed. Obedience would surely bring true peace and prosperity to the nation.

For the comfort of a remnant who will survive the exile, the LORD announces the day is coming when David's tabernacle (house) will again be established. We need to bear in mind that Amos is prophesying to the Northern kingdom where the king is not a son of David. That makes verse 11 all the more interesting, "On that day I will raise up the tabernacle of David, which has fallen down..." In other words, the hope of the covenant people of the North is in David. The Northern kingdom will disappear off the face of the map but the royal line of David will be established!

Under the rule of David and Solomon the territory of the kingdom had extended beyond the borders of Israel to include other nations and peoples. That is no longer the situation. The land of the inheritance has become a divided territory. Ten of the twelve tribes freed themselves from being under the dominion of the kings that were of the house and lineage of David.

Will the kingdom of David be restored physically to its former glory at some point in time? No! In fact, matters will get worse before they get better. The Northern kingdom of Israel will soon go into exile and Judah will also be taken into captivity. Foreign kings will rule over them. For centuries the throne of David will be vacant. The house of Jacob will be oppressed by the hand of a tyrant. When Jesus is born in Bethlehem, although He is of the house and lineage of David, He is not received as a prince but as a pauper. The glory of the house of David has departed from Israel.

The "tabernacle of David" signifies that which is flimsy and temporary. Over time it will collapse. Yet by the sovereign good pleasure of the LORD it will be made strong and glorious. The LORD will rebuild what has fallen to the ground. He will mend what has been torn apart by sin and disobedience. David's house has become like a building whose walls have caved in. The LORD promises to make it into a beautiful and majestic palace. It will be rebuilt to match its former glory. The LORD will fulfil what He said He would do despite the sins of this crooked and rebellious people. In Amos 9 the LORD reaffirms what He vowed to David in 2 Samuel 7, "Moreover I will appoint a place for My people Israel, and will plant them, that they may dwell in a place of their own and move no more; nor shall the sons of wickedness oppress them any more... Also the LORD tells you that He will make you a house. When your days are fulfilled and you rest with your fathers, I will set up your seed after you, who shall come from your body, and I will establish his kingdom. He shall build a house for My name, and I will establish the throne of his kingdom forever. I will be his Father, and he shall be my son... And your house and your kingdom shall be established forever before you. Your throne shall be established for ever"(2 Samuel 7:10, 11b, 12-14a, 16).

The LORD also reveals why He will establish the house of David. Amos 9:12 says, "that they may possess the remnant of Edom, and all the Gentiles who are called by My name..." Edom, was known to be the archenemy of Israel. The bitter rivalry that had begun in the days of Jacob and Esau continued throughout the generations. Earlier in the book of Amos, Edom was condemned because, "he pursued his brother with the sword, and cast off all pity; his anger tore perpetually, and he kept his wrath for ever" (1:11). The Edomites encouraged other nations to break down the walls of Jerusalem and to destroy the inheritance of Jacob. But now things are turned around. The house of David will be restored so that they may possess the remnant of Edom. The house of Jacob will be expanded to let in a remnant from Edom.

What is left of Edom will come under the rule of David. All the nations (Gentiles) that are called by the LORD'S name will be included in the inheritance and fall under the territory of David. In the LORD'S amazing grace He tells of the hope there is for a remnant of Edom – for Israel's arch-rival. The LORD will take a select number from the people of Edom and place them in the territory of His covenant. And if there is hope for them, there certainly will be hope for the remnant of Jacob as well.

The LORD is clearly referring to a future time – to events that were not realized in the Old Dispensation but which are being fulfilled today in the time after Christ's ascension and after the outpouring of the Spirit. From the time of Amos to the Babylonian captivity the nations did not come under the territory of David, but it is happening today because of David's great-grandson whom we know as our Lord Jesus Christ. With His ascension to the right hand of His Father's throne in heaven, the expansion of the territory begins and the boundaries of David's kingdom stretch across the whole world. Our Lord Jesus rules from David's throne in righteousness and equity. He fulfils what the angel Gabriel proclaimed to Mary before His birth, "He will be great, and will be called the Son of the Highest; and the LORD God will give Him the throne of His father David. And He will reign over the house of Jacob forever, and of His kingdom there will be no end"(Luke 1:32,33).

The restoration of David's tent is not by the initiative of people. The LORD is identified as the one who brings restoration. Our God and Father will restore the glory of the house of David through the work of His Son. Christ's kingdom will extend from sea to sea. He will gather the nations who are called by the name of the LORD.

The nations who are called by God's name are placed in a position of intimate oneness (Gen 48:16; 1 Kings 8:43). When a nation was "called by the name" of an individual it meant that it would come under his authority and ownership. 2 Samuel 12:26-28 gives us an incident that helps explains this. Joab, the commander of David's army, went out to battle against Rabbah of the Ammonites, and took the royal city. He sent a messenger to David saying, "I have fought against Rabbah, and I have taken the city's water supply. Now therefore, gather the rest of the people together and encamp against the city and take it, lest I take the city and it be called after my name." When David would take the city it would be under *his* authority and ownership.

In Deuteronomy 28:10, Moses tells Israel that the nations will see, "that you are called by the name of the Lord, and they shall be afraid of you." In the battle of the antithesis the Lord claimed Israel as His possession. They are under His authority, having been called by His name. Amos tells of a time which is coming when the Lord will broaden the scope. Thus this passage speaks powerfully of what Paul proclaimed in Eph 3:6, "...that the Gentiles should be fellow heirs, of the same body, and partakers of His promise in Christ through the gospel."

In the New Dispensation the Lord gathers a people who are called by His name from every nation and people on the face of the earth. In different words Amos proclaims the same message as Isaiah, "For unto us a Child is born, unto us a Son is given; and the government will be upon His shoulder. And His name will be called Wonderful, Counsellor, Mighty God, Everlasting Father, Prince of Peace. Of the increase of His government and peace there will be no end, upon the throne of David and over His kingdom, to order it and establish it with judgment and justice from that time forward, even forever. The zeal of the Lord of hosts will perform this" (Isaiah 9:6-7).

Our Lord Jesus establishes the house of David through His obedience. He accomplishes what David could not do. Sin threatened to destroy the kingdom of David and to take away any prospect of hope. And indeed, without Christ the house of David would have collapsed into ruin forever because a sinful kingdom cannot stand. Nevertheless, through Christ's sacrifice of atonement the kingdom will be restored and will come in its fulness.

The crucifixion, the resurrection of Christ, and the gathering of the church comprise the ultimate fulfilment of the words spoken by Amos. Who is the Son of David who now rules? Christ! Whereas the expansion of the kingdom David built was limited by geography, Christ's rule is ecumenical and universal. The great Son of David ascends to the throne of God and is given authority in heaven and on earth. It is through the apostolic ministry of His church – which is a ministry of the Word, of opening and closing the kingdom – that He gathers together those who are called by the name of the Father. We fall under His jurisdiction, rule, ownership and authority.

There are people who believe the restoration of the house of David will not take place until the thousand year reign of Christ – which they believe is still coming. On the basis of Revelation 20:1-6 they suggest Jesus will come down from heaven to rule on the literal throne of David over the present day people of Israel. As popular as such an interpretation may be among many Christians, it is based on speculation and conjecture and takes away from what Christ accomplished through His death, resurrection and ascension. It rolls back the clocks of redemptive time to the way things were in the Old Testament.

The apostle James sees the prophecy of Amos being fulfilled in the gathering of the church from both Jews and Gentiles. You can read about it in Acts 15. Having heard from the apostle Peter how the Lord is taking out of the Gentiles a people who are called by His name he says, "And with this the words of the prophets agree, as it is written [and then James gives a paraphrase of Amos 9], 'After this I will return and will rebuild the tabernacle of David, which has fallen down; I will rebuild its ruins, and I will set it up; so that the rest of mankind may seek the Lord, even all the Gentiles who are called by My name...'" (Acts 15:16,17).

The restoration of the house of David is through the ministry of Christ and manifests itself in the gathering of the church from different nations and people. The only demand that can be placed upon them is that they live by faith under their only King Jesus Christ. For through faith we have the assurance of God's continued blessing.

HOW DAVID'S HOUSE WILL BE BLESSED

Through Amos, the LORD also speaks about the blessings that will come with the restoration of the house of David. The message gets better. Verse 13 says, " 'Behold, the days are coming,' says the LORD, 'when the plowman shall overtake the reaper, and the treader of grapes him who sows the seed; the mountains shall drip with sweet wine, and all the hills shall flow with it.'" By means of images borrowed from farming Amos vividly portrays how the blessing of the covenant will be felt in all aspects of life. The harvest will be so abundant that the reapers will still be busy bringing in grain and grapes when the plowman is preparing the fields for the next crop.

Amos repeats the blessings of obedience as already stated in Leviticus 26:3-5. For there the LORD promised, "If you walk in My statutes and keep My commandments, and perform them, then I will give you rain in its season, and the land shall yield its produce, and the trees of the field shall yield their fruit. Your threshing shall last till the time of vintage, and the vintage shall last till the time of sowing; you shall eat your bread to the full, and dwell in your land safely."

In this picture the LORD portrays the blessings Christ will shower upon the people under His rule and government. The blessings of the covenant are *not* restored and established in the manner of the Old Testament, namely having Christ *physically* on earth in the city of Jerusalem. The scribes and Pharisees expected the Messiah to do this but they were wrong. Christ's kingdom is not to be thought of in an earthly manner. He has ascended to the throne of God and from *there* He promises to provide us with all things necessary for body and soul. This is the blessing you can expect when you walk in covenant obedience and keep the LORD's commandments. Christ promises to bless us from the heavenly Jerusalem (Galatians 4). The author to the Hebrews writes to Jewish Christians telling them not to expect blessing to come from the city of Jerusalem because as believers in Christ they have come to the heavenly Jerusalem (Hebrews 12).

The fulfilment of what was spoken by the prophet Amos will reach its climax when the Lord Jesus returns. At that time the New Jerusalem will come down from heaven and the Lord will complete His ultimate intention: to reclaim the entire world for Himself and

His glory. The blessings of wine and the incredible prosperity of bumper crops pictures poetically the abundance of life in the kingdom of heaven which we may experience today in part, and which will be granted to us in fulness on the new earth.

Another blessing of the restoration of the house of David is what we read in verse 14, "I will bring back the captives of My people Israel; they shall build the waste cities and inhabit them; they shall plant vineyards and drink wine from them..." When the LORD restores the fortunes of His people He changes their life situation. The LORD shifts from wrath to mercy and from destruction to blessing. Deuteronomy 30:3 says, "...that the LORD your God will bring you back from captivity, and have compassion upon you, and gather you again from all the nations where the LORD your God has scattered you."

Today we reap the harvest of Christ's rule in that we may share in His grace, mercy and love. We have peace in knowing that the LORD has restored the fortunes of His people. In the New Jerusalem there will no longer be any sin or the results of sin to plague us. We will be completely freed from the penalty of sin. The eternal inheritance will not be taken from us.

Amos also sees something of the redeemed condition of the church when he prophesies, "And no longer shall they be pulled up from the land I have given them." Through David's great son, Jesus Christ, the promises made to Abraham, Isaac and Jacob are fulfilled. The LORD calls a people to Himself, whom He will bless in every way, and who will dwell forever in the promised land. In Christ there is the assurance of a better day when all the blessings of the covenant will flow to us.

Therefore, even though we have heard much about judgment in this book and have been reminded of how we must worship the LORD according to the regulative principles of Holy Scripture, let us be encouraged to walk in the new obedience. The judgment we deserve came upon Christ. He paid the penalty of our sins.

The prophecy of Amos ends with five powerful words, "says the LORD your God." The LORD, your covenant God, has addressed you. He does not speak in generalities, but to you. You have heard what He criticizes and what He condemns. He has shown you from where you can expect His blessing and that true peace is found in obedience. The LORD has set you apart from all the families of the earth – yes, you only! Seek Him and live. In Christ we have the assurance that He will be everything to everyone.

Questions

1. The tone of the prophecy of Amos changes in verse 11 – sounding more positive and hopeful. What explains the sudden change?

2. What purpose does "the day of the LORD" serve (verse 11)? How does Amos' description of this day compare to what some of the other prophets have written?

3. The tabernacle of David which has fallen down will be raised up (verse 11). Why is it significant that the prophet speaks of the "tabernacle" of David and not the "throne" or "palace" of David?

4. If the message of Amos was heeded by any in the Northern kingdom of Israel, what course of action would they need to follow?

5. Look up Luke 2:36-38. To which tribe did the prophetess, Anna, belong? Where was she looking for redemption and consolation? Why is this passage so intriguing in view of Amos 9:11-15?

6. The prophets portray the exile as a return to the bondage of Egypt. Exile is a reversal of the gospel. Trace the imagery of "exile" or "captivity" in the book of Amos (4:2,3; 5:2,3; 5:27; 6:7;9:8,14). Note as well the references to Egypt.

7. Verse 11 announces a second exodus. How is this prophecy fulfilled?

8. Chapter 9:11-15 predicts both the birth of our Lord Jesus Christ and the outpouring of the Holy Spirit on the day of Pentecost. Discuss.

9. Who are the "Gentiles who are called by My name" (verse 12)?

10. Having studied the book in its entirety, list some of the main themes of this book. How do they assist you in serving the LORD today as members of Christ's church?

MAIN REFERENCES

1 Arnold, J.J. *Dingen die wij niet zien.* Goes:Oosterbaan & LeCointre, 1983.

2 Boice, J. M. *The Minor Prophets.* Grand Rapids: Kregel, 1986.

3 Calvin, J. *Calvin's Commentaries Volume XIV on the Minor Prophets.* Grand Rapids: Baker, reprinted 1979.

4 Dumbrell, William J. *The Faith of Israel: Its expression in the Books of the Old Testament.* Grand Rapids: Baker Book House, 1988.

5 Hasel, Gerhard F. *Understanding the Book of Amos: Basic Issues in Current Interpretations.* Grand Rapids: Baker Book House, 1991.

6 Hengstenberg, E. W. *Christology of the Old Testament.* Grand Rapids: Kregel, 1970.

7 Keil, C.F. and Delitzsch, F. *Commentary on the Old Testament in Ten Volumes Volume X.* Grand Rapids: Eerdmans, reprinted 1978.

8 Koch, Klaus. *The Prophets: The Assyrian Period.* Philadelphia: Fortress Press, 1987.

9 Limburg, J. *Hosea– Micah.* Atlanta: John Knox,1988.

10 Lok, P. *De Kleine Profeten.* Groningen: Vuurbaak.

11 Motyer, J.A.. *Amos: The Bible Speaks Today.* Downers Grove: Inter-Varsity Press, 1974.

12 Niehaus, Jeffrey. *The Minor Prophets: An Exegetical & Expository Commentary.* Grand Rapids: Baker Book House, 1992.

13 Ridderbos, J. *De Kleine Profeten* Vol I in de Korte Verklaring Der Heilige Schrift. Kampen: Kok, 1952.

14 Van Gelderen, C. *Het Boek Amos.* Kampen: Kok, 1933.

15 Veldkamp, Herman. *The Farmer from Tekoa.* St. Catherines: Paideia Press, 1977.

16 Vonk, C. *De Voorzeide Leer.* Hosea-Maleachi. Barendrecht: Liebeek & Hooijmeijer, 1983.

17 Wolff, Hans Walter. *Amos the Prophet. The Man and His Background.* Philadelphia: Fortress Press, 1973.

CPSIA information can be obtained at www.ICGtesting.com
Printed in the USA
LVOW082017230312

274520LV00001B/297/A